# Let us be Born:

## The inhumanity of abortion

By Mary Rosera Joyce
& Robert E. Joyce

Alethos Press

*Let us be Born*

Alethos Press
Div. of DGRCommunications, Inc.
Woodbury, MN

*Let us be Born: The inhumanity of abortion*
    Second Edition: By Mary Rosera Joyce, M.A.
    & Robert E. Joyce, PhD
    Editors: Russ Rooney and Dave Racer
    First Edition: By Robert E. Joyce, PhD and
        Mary Rosera Joyce, MA


ISBN Print Version: 978-0-9863773-4-1

ISBN eBook Version: 978-0-9863773-5-8

https://alethospress.com

Printed by VERSA Press, Inc., East Peoria, IL

# TESTIMONIALS

Human persons leap into existence "from zero to everything." This fact is beautifully shown in the book, *Let Us Be Born*. Philosopher, author and national treasure, Mary R. Joyce, now in her later years, still ponders the beauty of life and its intersection with science. Science explains many things, she notes, "Though some things that can be done should be done, not everything that can be done should be done. Otherwise, morality and civil law would be totally meaningless."

The beautiful and clear mind of Mary R. Joyce gave us a book the whole world should read: *Let us be Born*.

Alexandra Snyder, Esq.
Executive Director
Life Legal Defense Foundation

As I was reading through the book, especially Chapter 4, I couldn't help but catch my breath. The in-depth look at "Potential Human or Human Potential" defined for me the absolute beginning of life. I was

*Testimonials*

brought back to the moment when I learned of my mother's and father's choice to have a doctor place a needle in my mother's womb to extinguish me. The knowledge of the existence of my humanness, 'disrupting' their life, was the sole reason for trying to end my life. Their decision was driven by shame, convenience, and ignorance, not science.

Thankfully it didn't work. Here I AM...Same Human Full of Potential!

Melody A Olson
Survivor of Attempted Abortion

*Let us be Born* offers insight into the beginnings of the pro-life movement. These visionary leaders from Minnesota propose a base for beliefs still needed today which include aspects of science, philosophy, and faith—years before Roe v. Wade would become known as a landmark Supreme Court case."

Melanie A. Freimuth
Human Life Alliance Board President

# TABLE OF CONTENTS

*Let us be Born*

# FOREWORD TO THE 2020 EDITION

By Mary Rosera Joyce

> *"...there is no such thing as a potential human being, only a human being with potential."*
> –Chapter 4, *Let us be Born*

*Let Us Be Born* was originally published in 1970, nearly three years before the 1973 Roe v. Wade abortion decision. This book was the first grass-roots book of the American pro-life movement.

The cover shows a preborn child holding a sign that reads: 'Let Us Be Born.' This call for justice represents every child in the womb. It is the call made daily by the millions of Prolifers who continue to fight for the preborn's right to life, by their efforts in pregnancy counseling centers; in Prolife political efforts; at the various Marches for Life; and in our daily prayers for our preborn brothers and sisters.

Why is the pro-life movement taking so long to overcome abortion? Because the anti-life culture of death has taken hold of our society ever since the sexual revolution with its immature and selfish Playboy mentality that inevitably led to a demand for abortion. This was associated with moral relativism that denies there are objective moral norms based in the natural moral law.

Nonetheless, half a century later, some of the ideas in Let Us Be Born are catching on in a new generation, a generation of youth who realize they could have been aborted. These youth are thankful that their mothers respected their Right to Life.

## The Power of Language and the need for true morality

The power of language is being exploited by the abortion-culture: we have to counter it by using words to tell the truth.

This is the wisdom in our book's use of the positive word, 'preborn,' instead of the more negative sounding word 'unborn,' which tends to imply a child in the womb is like a non-being. Such an unsuitable word strikes the unconscious mind like an ax cutting a plant from its roots.

The word 'preborn' increases the power of the Prolife movement. So much depends on our use of words and images that shape our attitudes and culture. Prolifers need to counter the anti-life culture which preempted the language war by misusing American-sounding words like 'freedom of choice.' They even go so far as to say that an abortion of a handicapped child gives "a child the 'gift of peace' in preference to a life of suffering."

The pro-abortionists attack life by using the language of rights to accuse Prolifers of 'imposing our religious beliefs on women's right to choose' They ridicule Prolife values in this phrase which, like a sickle cutting grain, cuts down our values by reducing them to negative forces that violate the noble notions of a woman's freedom and rights.

Due to abortion, contraception and STD induced infertility, our population is now below the level needed to replace the present generation.

America is at a turning point where we choose between life and death. Will we continue to choose the 'political correctness' that leads to death? Or will we choose morality and restore the Right to Life for the survival of our nation?

## An Image and Likeness of God

According to Psalm 8:5 we are "a little less than the angels." But according to Roe v. Wade by the 1973 US Supreme Court we are lower than the animals, since they do not abort their young. It's time for women to become who they really are, not sex objects. And for men to become real men, not excuses for animals.

If women knew how they are, as Genesis says, an "image and likeness of God," how could they tolerate a so-called right of privacy to kill a preborn child?

Men and women are meant for the mind-and-heart sharing of friendship as the beginning of a true sexual revolution, based on our dignity as the image of the Triune God, Who is a Divine Communion of Persons. Man and woman are to become friends. Marriage and family are meant to image God's life and love.

–Mary Rosera Joyce

# DEDICATION COMMENTARY
By Russ Rooney

"To our brothers and sisters."

Robert and Mary Joyce first released this book in 1970, prior to the Roe v. Wade Supreme Court decision. They chose the dedication "To our brothers and sisters" then, and it remains apropos today. This book will help you understand the struggle to protect all human life prior to the legalization of abortion on demand. You will find that the Joyces were prophetic about how human life became discardable just three years after the book's publication.

It has been a pleasure for me to work with Mary and help her publish this book in the twilight of her life. Her late husband was a tremendous help to me when I wrote my own book, *Be a Friend for Life*.

Mary said that when she first heard the news of Roe v. Wade and Doe v. Bolton it sparked a light for life within her and since then she has remained engaged in the cultural battle to protect all human life. Mary has studied and used her wisdom to not only

*Dedication*

defend human life but also shed light on our relationship with God.

Bob was my philosophy professor at St. John's
University. There was no doubt that he was pro-life
and he showed his "pro-lifeness" through his words
and actions. He was a saintly giant both in stature and
intellect who gently passed away in 2014.

There are very few people in this world who
have done as much for the pro-life cause as Robert
"Bob" and Mary Joyce. Their observations in 1970 remain valuable today as we continue to fight for life.
Hence, most of the content in the first book has been
retained, with only few changes made with Mary's ap-
proval.

The importance of the prolife issue can be found
in this comment from a post-abortive woman: "Abortion was the only choice I was given. I didn't know
there were organizations that could help me. My heart
aches and I have a longing for my baby often. We deserve better. Babies and children deserve better."

Anyone who reads this book will finish it with
a better understanding of human dignity and the need
to defend all human life. Robert and Mary Joyce have
taught us the importance of our "being and meaning"
with words of truth.

–Russ Rooney, MLS
Author of *Be a Friend for Life*

# COMMENTARY

By Thomas W. Hilgers, MD

In the early 1970s, as I was beginning my residency in Obstetrics & Gynecology at the Mayo Graduate School of Medicine, I became extremely interested in the abortion issue. With that, I became also interested in the debate surrounding it. In the early days of my involvement, I picked up a small book titled *Let Us Be Born: The Inhumanity of Abortion* by Robert E. and Mary Rosera Joyce. This book is now being reprinted and I have been asked to write a foreward to it, which I am honored to do.

This book had an enormous effect on me when I was a young physician and the striking part of it to me was how so many new insights could be brought into what otherwise was a small book. I have since learned that Bob and Mary Joyce are very insightful philosophers who think deeply about life and relative associations to it. It is an extraordinary book using terminology and thought in ways that have affected me my whole professional life as I have looked at this issue. For example, they say that "… There is no such thing as a potential human being, only a human being with potential." The first part of that sentence is the argument that's often presented by those who are pro-abortion, but in reality, the truth lies in the second part of that statement.

Interestingly enough, I have just recently finished reviewing the transcripts of the arguments that were presented to the United States Supreme Court in the issues of Roe v. Wade and Doe v. Bolton. These were presented by the attorney general of the State of Texas and Sarah Weddington, the lawyer for the abortion movement. Throughout both of their arguments, the term, "potential human being" was used over and over and over again by Sarah Weddington. But even more astonishing – and truly exhibiting the lack of preparation for this argument – was the fact that the attorney general's office also continued to use the phrase, "potential human being" when referring to the preborn human person. And, in fact, Justice Blackmun himself used "potential human being" over and over in Roe and Doe. While I cannot prove this, it's only an intuition that I have, I sincerely believe that the use of that terminology by the state laid the groundwork, at least in part, for the two very famous abortion decisions of January 22, 1973.

The Joyce's discussion in Chapter 3 of "Conception – A Leap from Zero to Everything," is extraordinary and filled with insights that are logical and come from an intuition and knowledge on the science of human procreation. For example, they say:

Some pro-abortionists have been saying that the immediate result of conception is nothing more than a blueprint for the human person that is to come. But it takes very little reflection to realize how different a human zygote is from a non-living blueprint for a house. Unless it is used to paper the wall, a blueprint never becomes a part of the house. No house has ever been known to grow out of a blueprint like an organism. Again, this is a false reading of man-made things into natural development.

As a student of reproductive biology and medicine, it is true that the human zygote is the most important single human cell in all of human biology. It is far more potent than any stem cell that might be talked about and it is the originating cell of each and every human person. This is at times, difficult for people to imagine in their brains, but it's really not that complicated. An individual's human life begins at the moment that there is fusion of the sperm from the father and the ovum from the mother. A "leap from zero to everything," that is "from absolutely nothing of the forthcoming being to absolutely everything of that being – even though relatively everything about it is still to be developed." The famous German embryologist Bleschschmidt, in his study of embryology over 30 to 40 years, came to the same conclusion and he published it before Roe and Doe were released.

*Commentary*

The read you are about to embark upon in *Let Us Be Born: The Inhumanity of Abortion* is as relevant in 2020 as it was in 1970 when it was first published. The tragedy is that we as a culture have denied this for far too long. It is my hope that with the publication of this magnificent and yet small and very readable text, the reader will be as deeply impressed as I have been, and in fact, profoundly moved by it.

–Thomas W. Hilgers, MD
Clinical Professor
Department of Obstetrics and Gynecology
Creighton University School of Medicine
Director Saint Paul VI Institute for the Study of
Human Reproduction

*Dr. Hilgers is the author of The Fake and Deceptive Science Behind Roe v. Wade: Settled Law v. Settled Science." Beaufort Books in association with Saint Paul VI Institute Press, 2020.*

# FOREWORD–1970

By Juan J. Ryan

The lives of nations, like those of individuals, move slowly and almost imperceptibly to their desired ends. As a people is composed of many individuals, all in varying stages of life, all making their own moral choices, a pattern or tendency of action is difficult to perceive clearly from within. The observer himself tends to view only a small portion of the whole, and his views are influenced by the general trends of thought around him.

But every so often there appears in the life of a society or of a man a sudden and clear event, whose naked force portends the glory or the horror that is to come. Then for a moment the obscurity of our way is illumined as by a flash of lightning, and the road ahead may be clearly seen.

Just such an event was the sudden enactment this year by several of our states of statutes abolishing all criminal sanctions against abortion. The widespread contempt of a great number of our ruling class—legislators, publishers, and television commentators—for fetal human life has quickly become apparent. In a single stroke all the sanctions that protect the life of the new generation of mankind are done away with. Traditional morality and the role of law itself in protecting human life are thrown carelessly into the dustbin of history.

At the same time, our efforts to enact legislation to curb the injection of poisons into air, earth and water are turned against man himself. Man is the polluter, we are told; therefore we must, by abortion or any other means, prevent his numbers from increasing. Instead of punishing industrial establishments that befoul air and water, we are to praise those who do away with their unborn children. The polluters are men; therefore Man is our enemy. This illogical position is widely espoused by public men. One wonders whether this is not a gigantic death wish for mankind, and what will be its ultimate result. What if it becomes controlling in nations that possess the hydrogen bomb?

The inadequate food supplies of the poorer nations of the world are doubtless a pressing problem for them, and always have been, but they hardly seem to justify in the United States a national policy of reducing a birth rate which is now at the lowest point in our history. But in fact the argument of overpopulation is so used, and for a simple reason: Man is not regarded as having any intrinsic value. Human life is not considered to be created by God; it is a mere biological accident. This being so, abortion is but a little thing, and so are infanticide and euthanasia, for they remove from society its most helpless and dependent members. So far have we come in so little time.

But the battle for sanity and for humanity is not yet lost, and if it should be lost, it must be fought over again. The struggle of good and evil for the minds of men will go on to the end of time.

At this critical juncture, then, comes this book as a clarion call for justice for the helpless, the innocent, the unborn whose only crime is that, by the will of God of man, they came to be.

–JUAN J. RYAN, President
National Right to Life Committee
July 2, 1970

# INTRODUCTION (1970)

Though the words, "Let us be born" are not verbally expressed by the preborn child, they do articulate the nonverbal cry of his or her very being for life. One of the strongest tendencies in man is the desire to live. Human beings will go through great suffering in order to preserve their hold on life. Anyone who does not think that life is worth suffering for does not value it much. But love for life is essential to emotional and mental health. And anyone who loves life in himself surely will respect the right to life in others.

There is significant evidence that those who would easily dispose of preborn human beings have deep suicidal tendencies, sometimes unknown to themselves, and that they do not value their own lives authentically. It seems that many pro-abortionists suffer from an unconscious, if not conscious, despair. On the other hand, many of those who find abortion intolerable, not only for themselves but also for others, are people who have a great joy in being alive, and, as a result, cannot bear the destruction of prenatal human beings.

A most important part of a genuine sense of values in approaching the abortion issue is, then, a dynamic sense of gratitude for one's own life. We, too, need to be born and reborn in a love for life.

If we are to have an enlightened sympathy for the preborn child and his mother, sympathy implies emotional involvement. Enlightened sympathy implies a readiness to think complexly and profoundly about the facts of prenatal existence.

It has become fashionable to criticize all protest against abortion as being either emotional or coldly semantic and rational. But a merely emotional protest lacks the complexity of deep, perceptive reasoning. And cold rationality lacks the sympathy of involved feelings. Reason without emotion, and emotion without reason are both somewhat schizophrenic. So let us be born in a readiness to think with emotional involvement about life's beginning. Then, the nonverbal cry of the prenatal person, "Let us be born," will move us to respond in whatever way we can.

It is more than simply being emotional to assert that the contemporary abortion movement is one of the greatest atrocities in the history of man and woman. Far from being the warm, secure place that Freud claimed it was, the human womb is becoming, through our perverse use of technology, the most precarious locale of human life. People of good will everywhere are needed to speak out and to act on behalf of the poorest of the poor, the most undeveloped of our brothers and sisters. The fetal person is powerless to act effectively to protect himself or herself. All depends upon those who publicly take a stand as representatives of members of the human community who are still in life's first world, where each of us began to live and move and have our being.

# CHAPTER 1:
# WHAT IS THE SITUATION?

Until recently, many people have taken it for granted that abortion is the destruction of human life. But now the urgent clamoring for legal, hospitalized abortion has forced us to begin thinking, in depth, about the beginning of human life and the time when one human being actually lives in another. These things cannot be taken for granted any longer.

Furthermore, abortion is only one among many of the deeply critical issues involved in the ways that science, society and individuals will be able to control human life artificially in the near future. What should be our response to the scientist who eventually will attempt to cross cells from the human body with those of an animal so that a being with the best features of the human and lower animal forms might be produced? When does human life begin? When does it come to an end? To ask these questions, and many others of their kind, is to confront the very meaning of the human person.

The time is coming when man will be able to make himself over in some ways. But with his developing techniques of biochemical engineering, what is

1

the kind of life that he would seek to produce? Should man try to make himself over or to evolve directly by self-manipulation? Is he meant, instead, to evolve indirectly by improving his environment? At present, most of the human potential is not developed due to environmental restrictions. As we improve our environment, we develop our potential and increase the quality of life much less forcibly and dangerously than by such procedures as genetic surgery. Furthermore, if air, water, soil and food pollution continue, we will lose the most basic conditions for life, to say nothing of its quality. What, then, is the relation of technology to the human person? This is one of the most serious questions confronting our sense of values today.

Ever since Descartes divided man into a mind and a machine, science has been turned loose on the "machine," man's body. Many benefits have resulted, particularly in the science of medicine. But ironically, scientific technology has continued also to dehumanize the person. In fact, if man is a mind in a machine he is not even a person to begin with. A person is a being whose powers are all integral to one another. But the dualism of a mind and a machine depersonalizes man and leaves him vulnerable to exploding research in technology and medicine almost for their own sake.

One result is that abortion is now among the simplest and "safest" forms of surgery, and many are urging that it be treated simply as a medical matter no different from the removal of tonsils or appendix.

When utilitarian values become deeply rooted and widely accepted, people tend to think that whatever man can do for his own convenience, he should do. Because abortion can be simply and safely done they tend to think that it should be allowed. But morality as well as civil law is based upon a real difference between can and should. Though some things that can be done should be done, not everything that can be done should be done. Otherwise, morality and civil law would be totally meaningless.

Facing the problem of abortion is not merely a matter of inquiring into the methods of performing the operation, nor of gaining more accurate statistics on the number of abortions, nor of properly interpreting popular-opinion polls on the subject. The greatest need is to focus upon the most relevant and urgent questions involved. Abortion is not so much "the problem of unwanted pregnancy" as it is a raising of the question whether pregnancy is a relationship between two human beings, one dwelling within the other.

## A Religious Issue?

Those who are determined to separate state law from religious values ought to recall that the Ten Commandments forbid lying, stealing, murder and other violations of the human person. These Biblical imperatives are religious values, but they are also human social values. The social principle, "Do to others as you would have them do to you," is a humanistic, as well as Christian, principle. In the case of abortion, the others are the preborn, conceived by a human father and a human mother. There is much that can be understood about these prenatal beings and their rights without an appeal to religious values. In a society where religious values are extremely diverse, and where these exist together with agnostic and atheistic attitudes, the strongest court of appeal for the fetal person is the value of the individual human life itself. A society that forsakes this value, at any stage of human existence, implies, even if it does not practice it immediately, that all human beings could be regarded as disposable things.

On the other hand, religious beliefs, or the lack of them, definitely are influential in a society. They can be influential, however, without being imposed. Even if the abortion issue were a religious matter, the law should be decided on other than religious grounds. Suppose some religious group decided to sacrifice the life of one innocent child a month as part of its worship services. Would the state be obliged to protect the so-called freedom of religion in this case? No! Civil society cannot be a valueless society.

Though the foregoing example may seem strange, perhaps it can be shown that, in our society today, responsible family planning and creative alleviation of social problems are being corrupted by a kind of "humanistic" religion which advocates sacrificing to the gods of human convenience and pleasure any innocent human life that gets in the way. All that is necessary is to incense the offering so that the smoke of rationalization keeps the true identity of the victim hidden from public notice. Is the state supposed to protect the so-called freedom of this "religion?"

The abortion issue reaches into the depths of a society's moral foundations. It is not simply a medical issue; it is legal, ethical, psycho-social, and above all philosophical—in the sense of involving the very meaning and value of human existence on this planet and in this universe. In some way, public philosophy and morality are defined in medical and legal practice, in legislative statutes, and generally, in every kind of social structure. Evaluation of present laws and opinion-trends on abortion can lead us, if we are honest, into the very nerve center of a genuinely pluralistic society, one that is pluralistic enough to include the rights of its prenatal members.

## Freedom or Tyranny?

If we consider deeply enough the evidence in all the relevant areas of research, we will see that abortion is really tyrannical, and that this tyranny can easily pass under the guise of freedom. It is based on discrimination and utility, rather than on equality and freedom. For the sake of a genuine liberty in society, we need to discern which laws are subject to compro-

- guise of freedom
discrimination + utility
Not equality + freedom

mise and which are not. In matters where there is a middle ground, or a question of degrees, compromise might be acceptable. Since there is no middle ground between life and death, there are no grounds for compromise on innocent human life. A broken arm can be healed. Even a ruined reputation can be restored. But a human being cannot be returned from death. Only a false sense of liberty will suggest that all laws are subject to compromise–liberty of this type ends where the right to life begins.

Is the defense of the preborn a matter of imposing our views on others? It is being said that many people do not believe abortion is the killing of a human being, and that these people should have the freedom to follow their opinions, especially if they are, or become, the majority in our society. It is being said that the beliefs of the Catholic Church should not be forced upon everyone.

Aside from the fact that reducing the abortion question to a controversy of Catholic versus non-Catholic is religious bigotry of the basest kind, since many non-Catholics also oppose legalized abortion, the question must be asked whether the state can act on mere opinion in this matter. No one has proved that the human zygote, embryo or fetus is not a human being. There is no scientific evidence that plant life or mere animal life is conceived by a human father and a human mother. In fact, scientific evidence shows that a new human being begins to develop at conception, and that at that moment, this new life has everything necessary for becoming a human adult except nourishment and nurture.

It might be asserted that the state acts on opinion no matter what stand it takes on prenatal life. But the weight of the evidence is certainly on the side of the opinion that human life begins at conception. Once conception takes place, it is a proven fact that normally a baby will be born nine months later, a fantastically short time considering the years of growth and development that follow birth. Since no thoughtful person would deny the possibility that a human being exists at conception, we must act on the basis of this great possibility, and not on the basis of the opinion that is only founded on scientific evidence.

Regarding the opinion that certain human organisms are not human beings, we need to recall that the Nazi scientists did not view the Jews as being human, but only as being part of nature. With our armies and Allies we forced them to abandon their dehumanizing experiments on these people, and their deathcamps as well. During the years of slavery in the South, and even afterward, many did not regard the blacks as human beings. Yet the North forced the South to abandon slavery. In these and similar matters, opinion is likely to be a rationalization for the sake of vested interests, rather than a result of unbiased study and observation. Someone is needed to take a stand for the humanity of the oppressed.

## *What is the Situation?*

Recently many people have thought that black and brown people have imposed their desire for equality upon white people, that our government has imposed civil rights laws on our society. But even if the majority opinion of the whites had been opposed to civil rights laws, our government would have been justified in imposing the equality of minorities upon the majority. Concerning human equality, especially in the right to life, we cannot maintain our Constitution without imposing certain basic values upon the society. Our Declaration of Independence—the document through which we view the Constitution—states that "all men are created equal" and are endowed by their Creator with certain inalienable rights, the first being the right to life. This means the lives of the weakest and most defenseless among us (including the preborn) are as deserving of protection as the most powerful, including the President, the Justices of the Supreme Court and the Legislators.

Might does not make right! If the strong do not defend the weak, and we are all weak in one way or another, civilization cannot long endure.

# CHAPTER 2:
# OUR BROTHERHOOD
# WITH THE PREBORN

By realizing that we have much in common with our prenatal brothers and sisters, we can enlighten and increase our concern for their welfare. Their rootedness, growth and transitions are not unlike our own.

At first, the child is physically located and then rooted in his mother. After the transition of birth, he or she is emotionally, as well as physically, rooted in her love and care. The physical umbilical cord is cut at birth, and the emotional connection gradually recedes as the child becomes somewhat independent in his or her thoughts and feelings. But in all stages of his life, he or she remains rooted in the womb of the world.

In order to realize how rooted the child is, the adult need only imagine himself or herself with no ground beneath their feet, no gravity to hold them there, no air to breathe, food to eat, water to drink, and nothing to see, hear, touch, taste or smell.

## We are All in a Womb

The atmosphere of the earth is like the amniotic fluid in the mother's womb. Both are protective. Without the earth's atmosphere, we could be struck by meteorites at any time, and there would be temperatures of 240 degrees above and below zero. The astronaut suspended outside his space capsule and attached to this "little earth" with an umbilical cord, is a graphic proof that man is rooted in the womb of mother nature.

The embryo-child grows in the womb of his or her mother; the embryo-adult grows in the womb of the world. Though adults are not physical embryos, they may be embryos emotionally, mentally and spiritually. It has been scientifically discovered that only a small percentage of the brain potential of the human adult is ever developed. With our continuing wars, violence, hatred and jealousies, how much have we evolved emotionally since the cave man? Embryonic as we are, in view of the vast potential latent in our being, anyone who destroys the life of an adult likewise aborts that person from the womb of this world.

Sometimes the life in the womb is described as parasitic. But we are all parasitic in being deeply attached to the womb of society. Which one of us makes his own clothes, cultivates his own food, builds his own shelter and supplies his own medical care? We depend on society not only for the fulfillment of these

10

basic needs but also for education and methods of travel. Furthermore, the child or adolescent, in her dependence upon her parents, might be regarded as parasitic until her college education is finished. This profound dependency is part of the human condition; it is not reserved for the prenatal child.

## Life is a Series of Births

Human life is a continuing series of births. The fetus becomes an infant; the infant becomes a toddler and preschooler; the schooler is born from his or her home into the wider community of the classroom; through the birth-trauma of adolescence, the self emerges anew. Even in adulthood there are transitions from youth to middle age to old age, each marked by a sense of moving into a new world. Finally, death is a kind of birth into a new world. And before this birth takes place, an adult knows as little of the next world as the fetus knows about the earth before he or she moves into its environment.

Only a superiority complex can make us think that we are persons and the preborn are not. A great difference in size and developed ability makes one no less, nor more, a person than the other. It is true that the preborn do not seem to have a personality, but the meaning of person is not the same as the meaning of personality. As the infant responds to, and identifies with other people around him, he or she develops their

11

personality. But if she were not a person to begin with, she could not develop a personality. As the science of fetology advances, it might become possible to discern, in the tiny person, the beginnings of the personality that eventually will develop.

For all practical and legal purposes, not to decide whether the human zygote, embryo or fetus is a person is to decide that he or she is not. Decision is inevitable. The challenge of proof is mainly for those who are ready to claim that the prenatal being is not human. In view of the highly advanced contemporary knowledge of the generative process, the consequences of terminating innocent human life ought to put massive pressure upon the pro-abortionist to produce scientific evidence that the human conceptus is not a human being, and therefore not equally valuable with his or her mother and others in postnatal society. The attitude that should prevail is, at least, that the human zygote is a human person until proven otherwise. Especially in a society such as our own, where a person is innocent until proven guilty, a being conceived by a human father and mother should be regarded as a human person unless conclusively proven to be something else. But who can prove that a human being does not exist at the beginning of his or her own growth?

# CHAPTER 3: CONCEPTION– A LEAP FROM ZERO TO EVERYTHING

According to powerful scientific evidence, the life-thrust and genetic characteristics for the fully developed adult are present in the first cell that results from the union of sperm and ovum. The growth that follows is not just a spreading of protoplasm, or a simple multiplication of cells. From the very beginning, a special organization and differentiation of parts is evident. After six weeks of development, all the internal organs of the human being are present. At nine weeks, the hands and feet are almost as beautiful as they are in the newborn. Yet pro-abortionists call this being a glob of protoplasm or a knot of cells. They can do this only by completely turning off the evidence. This is not only a matter of an unwanted pregnancy, but also of unwanted evidence.

Those who think that human organs are formed before a human being comes into existence are misinterpreting a basic fact of nature. Only man-made things come into existence part by part. Natural beings may develop stage by stage, but they do not come into existence that way; they come into existence all at once. As one scientist has described the beginning of a new species in evolution, the beginning of a new being at conception is also "a leap from zero to everything." Though his or her parts are not yet fully expressed, a whole new human being is there, and they manifest their fully given reality by growing. Only a human being can develop a human brain. A human brain cannot develop before a human being exists. And a human brain begins to develop soon after conception. In fact, the brain is the first organ to begin developing.

The great difference between a living being and a man-made thing is that the living being is a dynamic cause in its own development, whereas a man-made thing is not. An organism develops itself, but a table, book or clock does not develop itself. From the very beginning of its growth, the living being that is developing is present as the principal cause in its own growth.

When people imagine that a living being must develop to a certain extent before it can exist, they are obviously reading into nature the way they themselves make tools or other artifacts. But mankind greatly falsifies its understanding by projecting its own way of making things into its interpretation of nature's way of developing organisms. Even great philosophers like

Aristotle and Thomas Aquinas were victims of this artifact-projection. Aristotle thought that a certain amount of biological formation was necessary before human life began. He thought that it took 40 days of development before the male became human, and 80 days before the female became human. Aquinas accepted this without modification. Aside from the obvious male prejudice in such a view, neither of these men had anything like the evidence of modern science on which to base their judgments. But pro-abortionists are fond of quoting them, while any reference to modern science often is noticeably absent. According to scientific evidence, everything that is needed for a human adult, except nourishment and nurture, comes into existence at conception. But we moderns are looking into the electron microscope and simply refusing to admit what we see—the evidence that a human individual begins at conception. We are more unfortunate than those later Medieval sages who refused to look into the telescope to see the unwanted evidence that the sun, rather than the earth, is the center of the solar system. Aristotle and Thomas Aquinas would have been first to look and admit what they saw, not only through the telescope, but also through the high-powered microscopes we have today.

Some pro-abortionists have been saying that the immediate result of conception is nothing more than a blueprint for the human person that is to come. But it takes truly little reflection to realize how different a human zygote is from a non-living blueprint for a house. Unless it is used to paper the wall, a blueprint never becomes part of the house. No house has ever been known to grow out of a blueprint like an organism. Again, this is a false reading of human-made things into natural development.

The human zygote is much more than a "genetic package," or a bundle of genes. It is a living being that has genes. We do not think that an adult person is a package of organs, muscles and bones, but that he or she is a being who has organs, muscles and bones. There is a secondary sense in which the person is his organs and other parts, but he is always much more. With any organism, and especially with a person, the whole is always much more than the mere sum of its parts.

Though the human being in the zygotic stage of life does not have the familiar shape of the human body, it would be scientifically naive to judge solely by what she does not appear to have. Judging by appearances, after all, we would think falsely that the sun moves around the earth.

## I Am a Developed Zygote!

There are some who think that the human being comes from a zygote, or from the unique union of an ovum and sperm. It is much more accurate, however, to think that the adult person actually is a developed zygote. Rather than saying that a human comes from a child, it is more accurate to say that he or she is a developed child. Just as I came from these parents without being these parents, I came from this ovum and sperm without being this ovum and sperm. But once the ovum and sperm united, there I am! The new one-celled reality is not something that I come from, but is my being. There is a certain kind of sophisticated adult who would refuse to admit that she once was a single-celled being. Such an acknowledgment actually requires humility.

Because our reality-awareness is so undeveloped, we are trapped very often by the usual meanings of the words we use. For instance, it is quite easy to become trapped by the term "comes from." Just as it is mistaken to think that the sun literally rises in the east and sets in the west, it is mistaken to think that a human being comes from any one of his or her stages of development. Even as it is truer to think that our location on earth is moving around to face the sun or to turn away from it, so it is much more crucially true to say that the human zygote is an undeveloped person who comes from a specific human sperm uniting with a specific human ovum. The point is that the united ovum and sperm is neither an ovum nor a sperm; it is an actual, though undeveloped, human being. And this new being is no less human for being undeveloped. Thus, while it is an improvement to say, "I am a developed zygote" it is still not wholly accurate. It would be best to assert with reflection: just as I was once a child, or a somewhat developed, but fully human, being, I was once a zygote or a relatively undeveloped, but fully human, being.

Even in the case of parthenogenesis (an ovum developing without fertilization by a sperm) the new being exists with the initiation of the process before the division from a one-celled to a double-celled unit. The new being is the principal cause in its own development and is sustained in its growth by proper environmental conditions and stimuli. Otherwise it is some kind of artifact. (According to Christian teaching, Jesus was conceived in a parthenogenic manner by the power of the Spirit, and He came into existence as the Son of God at the moment of conception.)

**An Acorn is an Oak Tree**

It is easy, but naive, to say that an acorn is not an oak tree, and to imply, by saying this, that a human zygote or embryo is not a human being. Especially for a highly sophisticated biologist, it is scientifically naive to say that an acorn, specifically in its fertilized core, is not an oak tree, just a potential oak tree. The fertilized portion of an acorn IS an undeveloped oak tree, but an oak tree nevertheless. Does a thing have to be developed before it can BE? Again, we are trapped in words. If the fertilized part of the acorn is not an undeveloped oak tree, when does the oak tree begin to exist as such? When it is an inch tall, or three feet tall, or only when it is ready to produce seeds? If we take the word "oak tree" too seriously, we are inclined to think that a thing is an oak tree only when it is more or less fully grown. In that case, the word "human being" would have to mean "man or woman." An infant, toddler, young boy or girl would not be considered human beings. It is much more reasonable to assert that fertilization is a "leap from zero to everything," that is, from absolutely nothing of the forthcoming being to absolutely everything of that being—even though relatively everything about it is still to be developed.

Though its roots, trunk and branches are not yet expressed within itself, the dynamic being of the oak tree is present as the fertilized portion of the acorn. Even when these parts are developed, they are internal revelations in space and time of the very being of the tree that was fully present at the beginning of its own growth. The oak tree has the potency to develop roots, trunk and branches. The potency to develop these members does not pre-exist the oak tree itself; to think so is simply to "put the cart before the horse." And even when the oak tree has developed roots, trunk and branches, it is something much more than all of these self-expressions. The whole is greater than the sum of its parts. Before developing any of its parts, this same whole is greater than its potency to develop all its parts. If an oak tree were only the sum of its parts, it would have to be a man-made thing, an artifact like a table, chair, cupboard, or wristwatch. The great difference between something that is hand-made or put together from the outside, and something that manifests its own being from within, cannot be overemphasized.

# CHAPTER 4:
# A POTENTIAL HUMAN, OR A HUMAN WITH POTENTIAL?

Following conception by a human father and a human mother, what is it that takes in nourishment and grows, while having everything needed to become a human adult? Is it just a potential human being? But what about the scientific evidence that only about five percent of the brain potential of the normal adult is ever realized? It seems that adults, too, are only potential human beings. Pro-abortionists continue to use the expression "potential human being" in referring to life in the womb, but not one of them has explained precisely what they mean by "potential." Invariably, they assume that a person cannot exist before any of his or her potential is developed.

But at conception, with the existence of the one-celled zygote, the most important of all realities of the human person is fully developed. This is the reality of his or her being. The zygote is the very being of the human person, a being that has a unique genetic dynamism, a being without which there is no other human potentiality. Potentiality can exist only in this kind of actuality; the actuality of an individual being. The human zygote is a unique self. All the human potentialities actually exist, though in an undeveloped manner, in this single-celled person.

## The Potential Actually Exists

The zygotic self cannot actually breathe, but he actually has the undeveloped capacity for breathing. Nor can this zygotic self actually think and love as an adult does, but she actually has the undeveloped capacity for thinking and loving. And the human zygote could not actually have such undeveloped capacities unless he or she actually IS the kind of being that has such capacities. Just as it is obviously true that only a human being can have the developed capacities for thinking and loving, it should be obviously true that only a human being can have the undeveloped capacities for thinking and loving. The one-celled horse, dog or goat has no such undeveloped capacities; thus, they have no such developed capacities. The one-celled dog, for example, is qualitatively different from the one-celled human, not only in genetic structure, but much more basically in the very being that has a particular genetic structure.

The dignity and value of the human being is not determinable simply on the basis of what he or she actually has, but on the basis of what he or she actually is. The value of the person is not primarily in their actualities that have come to term, but most radically in the actuality of what he or she IS. And his or her being always has undeveloped potential, no matter how long and active their life on earth may be.

## Two Kinds of Potential

People who claim that the life in the womb is merely a potential human being fail to distinguish two radically different kinds of potency. The first kind is that of the ovum and sperm separately—the potency to cause something to come into being. Neither the ovum nor the sperm, nor the two together, is a potential human being. These germ cells have only the potency to cause a human being.

The second kind of potency is that of the zygote: the potency to become fully what it IS. Thus, there is no such thing as a potential human being, only a human being with potential. (See the Appendix on Page 93 for a more detailed explanation of the different kinds of potency.)

Since the zygote is not an ovum in any sense, the expression "fertilized ovum" can be very misleading. The zygote comes into being through the causality of the matter and structure of the ovum. But no matter how much it may look, in its form and be-havior, like an ovum, it is not an ovum. Radically, its form and behavior are that of an entirely new kind of being. A zygote is not an ovum plus a sperm, as a table is a flat surface plus legs. The organic whole (the zygote) is far greater than the mere sum of its parts. It IS much more than it has.

## Person and Being

Because some people tend to think that a being must either look like a person or act like a person in order to be a person, they find it impossible to understand that the human zygote is a human person. With either a biological or psychological definition of person, they are hopelessly trapped in parts of a whole, and fail to perceive the totality involved. The biological definition of the person is usually based on physical shape and function. And the psychological definition is based on some kind of self-awareness, or ability to reason, or enculturated personality. But being is much more basic in meaning than the form or actions of a thing. The human zygote does not even have a brain, but the very being of the human brain, or the capacity to develop a human brain, is actually present in the human zygote. Confronted with the impact of being, both the biological and psychological definitions of the human person are basically inadequate.

Though some people with a biological or psychological meaning for the person try to argue that a human person is not present at conception, they cannot

24

succeed in showing that a human being is not present at conception. The very force of being immediately undermines their arguments. But the human being is always a human person. The meaning of person demands an ontological (being-based) definition, while including biological and psychological aspects.

It is possible, then, for a human person to exist, as a person, before any of his members or powers are developed. In fact it is necessary. What a natural organism can become, it already IS—in an absolute way. An undeveloped person is no less a person. Even the adult is more potentiality than actuality.

Though a beautiful actress has much more personality and charisma than her infant son or daughter, she is no more a human person than her child. Nor, for that matter, would she be any more a person than her newly conceived child. The child has just as much right to develop a personality as the mother has to express her developed personality.

## What is a Person?

Only some beings are persons. Why is a human being a person, and an animal not so? A person is a being who can become aware of his own existence; he can say "I." And, in being able to say "I" he can also say "You" and "We." As a result of this basic, but highly creative, awareness, he can begin to ask questions and try to work out their answers; he can develop the process of reasoning. But the danger of taking this meaning too psychologically cannot be overstated. Any being who has the potential for developing this self-awareness, even if "only" a human zygote, is actually a person.

However, someone easily might try to argue that the person does not exist at any time before he knows it. "How can I say that I existed before there was even an I to know this?" It is so easy to assert that actual self-awareness is the quality making a person exist. A child becomes aware of herself as an "I" only around the age of two or two and a half years. People rarely, if ever, have memories that date back into their first or second year. Are they only potential persons before that time? If so, a woman in a deep coma who does not know, and who might never know again, that she exists, could be regarded as a potential person. And since she does not seem to be able to come to self-awareness again, she might even be thought to be less than a potential person. The same could be thought about a mental patient who does not know who he or she is anymore. Someone might begin to think that it takes more than a human shape to be a person, and that the biological processes in these human shapes might be mercifully terminated. But then the human shape under anesthesia on an operating table would not be safe from this termination complex. None of us, while sleeping, has actual self- awareness. The similarity between a sleeping adult, particularly if he is lying in a fetal position, and the child in his mother's womb, is really striking. And it could be frightening. Many people use sleep as a therapeutic "escape" from reality, or even as a kind of retreat to the comfort of the womb. But now we are forced to realize that not even the womb is a safe place anymore.

In order to see more clearly the logical consequences of misunderstanding the meaning of the person, the following example is constructed.

## A Letter from One Humanist to Another

The report in a national paper regarding your generous care of women who want to terminate their pregnancies has been called to my attention. I am very interested in the prospects of such humanism for the future. Eventually it will not be enough just to ensure that any woman who wants an abortion has it safely done. The need to curb population growth and to develop quality in human life is becoming more urgent every day.

Recently it has occurred to me that there is a great need to develop a definition of human life such that humanists can begin a strong movement toward the development of human quality. Until now, many people have been thinking only in terms of a biological meaning for the human organism. On this basis they have come to see that the organism in the womb is not a human being because it is not yet breathing, or separated from its mother. Thus, they have accepted abortion as a method of birth control. But it seems to me that a psychological rather than a biological definition of the human being would be much more proportionate to the nature of the being himself.

According to an experiment with the reactions of a human baby and those of a young monkey, it was not possible to say at what moment a truly human intelligence began to appear. But it was obvious that in three or four years the human baby was different. On the basis of such experimental evidence, a good psychological definition of the human being might well exclude babies up to three years of age or so. Since many babies that are wanted at birth become unwanted children before they are three years old, either because they are physically or psychologically damaged by that time, or because of unforeseen conditions in the environment, these, too, might be harmlessly removed from society by some kind of medically administered injection. All mental defectives, including the retarded, psychotic and severely neurotic could also be excluded by a good psychological definition of human life.

Finally, we will have to take the next and

ultimate step by developing a sociological definition of the human person. Man is so obviously a social being. On the basis of this most advanced definition, we will be able to see that society has just as much right to dispose of any unwanted or burdensome members as the mother has to dispose of an unwanted pregnancy.

The ever-increasing burden of social security taxation eventually will meet with the taxpayer's rebellion. If the living tissue in the mother's womb can be regarded as parasitic matter to be removed when unwanted, what about the parasitic tissue in the womb of society? All of those who are dependent upon social security for existence, or dependent on social welfare of some kind, are really parasites living off the resources of others. Unproductive consumers are becoming an increasing, soon to be intolerable, burden on the productive consumer. Why can they not be treated as simply medical matters and harmlessly removed? A precise and highly specified sociological definition of man would exclude all human tissue that is parasitic in its maintenance.

Now, the day is bound to come when you and I will be subjected to these more proportionate definitions of human life. You and I might have to be removed from the womb of society in a harmless medical procedure. But we will be enlightened enough to know that this treatment is necessary not only for the quality of society, but also for its health and survival. At first, people will say that this is a return of the Nazi attitude toward a quality race. But by that time most of the members of society will be ready to accept what was good and reasonable in the Nazi movement.

Best wishes for success in your efforts to humanize this planet.

Sincerely, H. F. (Humanist of the Future)

Anyone who thinks that the writer of this letter is ahead of his time ought to consider the words of a representative in the Arizona legislature who recently introduced a bill to restrict family tax exemptions for the purpose of population control. In his written appeal to his fellow committee members he said that very soon adults may have to decide how long they want to live. As he put it, they might have to ask, "When must I decide I shall die?" The most ominous word in this phrase is must.

## Dualism Again!

Any reasoning about the human person that opposes his biological and psychological processes is dangerously separatistic. It is basically Cartesian and Manichaean in its sources. Descartes with his dualistic mind and machine, and the Manichaeans with their dualistic spirit and matter have sinned against the truth of the human person. They have degraded man by seriously violating the profound unity of his total being. And contemporary existentialists have done little better. What have they accomplished by identifying existence with human awareness and saying that everything other than human awareness does not even exist? Everything else might be there, but none of it exists. Sartre is the supreme Manichaean of the existentialists.

To assume that man is anything other than a radical unity of being that transcends, while profoundly including, his biological and psychological processes is to court the ancient and ever-tempting dualism that plagues our understanding of ourselves. It is quite easy for the human mind to fall into a kind of metaphysical schizophrenia. Even the greatest thinkers of history were afflicted by this disease. Now, more than ever, in an age of rampant technology, the implications of dualistic thinking are becoming practical and affecting our everyday lives. Reinforced by a utilitarian ethic, the consequences will be terrifying.

**The Question of Evolution**

Dualistic thinking is also prevalent in those who

think that the human embryo must develop a human shape before the soul is infused to take over the body. They fail to realize how similar this would be to making a motor, pouring gasoline into it, and then starting the motor. No! Man's way of making and operating machines is not nature's way of conception and development. Organisms begin with all their parts existing together in an implicit manner; growth is the internal revelation of the being that is fully present in its own conception.

Nor is it acceptable to think that conception is followed by an evolution from a plant-type of organism to an animal-type before it finally becomes a human being. How could a plant-type of being have the genetic dynamism of a human being? And while this so-called "plant" is developing a so-called "animal" shape, does it have only a plant-type soul? How can a thing with a plant soul be developing an animal shape? This is, again, the artifact-type of thinking, reading man's way of making things into his interpretation of a developing organism.

It is true that the human zygote looks like a plant-type of organism. And there is a time when the embryo and fetus look like various forms in the animal kingdom. But there are adult persons who also have striking resemblances to subhuman creatures. A being is not always what it looks like. There is a sense in which individual development in the womb (ontogeny) recapitulates the evolution of species (phy-

32

logeny). But this recapitulation is not literal, or identical with the evolution of species. It is only similar. And there is a profound difference between the identical and the similar. If the beginning of a new kind of being in the evolution of species is a "leap from zero to everything" and not a gradual process at all, no less is true concerning the beginning of each being within a species. It is as false to say that the offspring of human parents is ever simply vegetative or sentient in nature as to say that a computer "thinks and feels."

Because we think of man as evolving from animal life, it may seem reasonable to hold that the human zygote passes through an animal stage of development before it becomes human. But as the hand comes from the whole person, in and through his arm, man evolved from the total energy of creation, in and through the animal kingdom. When the time was ready, the basic energy of the human person absorbed into itself, and completely transformed into itself, the energy of animal life. Thus, there never was a moment when man was an animal, or had an animal body. No less is true for the evolution that goes on in the human zygote, embryo and fetus.

There is nothing in a human that intuitively belongs to an animal, or that is an animal form or function. Everything in a human belongs to a person and is fully personal in nature. Thus, it is false to define humans as rational animals; he or she must be defined, if at all, on the basis of his or her personhood. Man is

33

animal-like, even as he is God-like. But he is in no sense an animal, as he is in no sense God. And he comes into existence as a human person before the first division of the cell that results from conception. Otherwise he is some kind of artifact or likeness of man-made things.

## The Problem of Twinning

But some people think that the formation of identical twins argues against the existence of the human being at conception. They rightly insist that the growing zygote which divides in half cannot be viewed as one human being dividing into two. But the result of twinning is similar to what scientists are now saying about the possibility of inducing generation in an ordinary cell of the adult's body, and developing an identical twin for that person. The adult from whom the cell is taken would be the only parent of his twin. In a somewhat similar manner, the original zygote, a human being, becomes a parent of another in twinning, though it is more difficult, in this case, to identify the parent.

There is evidence, too, that in these first days of life, twins or triplets sometimes "recombine" into a single individual, (e.g., Cf. Andre Hellegers, "Fetal Development," Theological Studies, March, 1970.) Should this fact be interpreted as evidence that an irreversible individual does not exist for some days after conception? As twinning is a creation of a new individual, the reversal of this process by mergence is the death of one of the new beings and the survival of the other—one of the various ways in which human beings are subject to an extremely early natural death. This phenomenon of recombination probably means that one of the individual beings absorbs the other, which would mean the death of that other. Such an absorption need not imply a lack of individuality, but rather, an instability in the physical organization of the individual at this early stage of development.

In any event, there is at least one unique individual (if not two or more) actually existing at conception or fertilization. Our inability to determine the exact number of individual persons in these cases should not obscure our sacred duty to assist and preserve, through whatever resources are available, the unique human life that is present at conception.

## The Problem of Tissue Culture

The complex matter of human tissue culture provides a more subtle area for doubting the absolute beginning of the person at conception. Preserving and multiplying human cells in certain nutritive fluids long after the person has died is an intriguing endeavor of biological science that already has proven successful. If the cells of a person can live and multiply in test tubes long after the person is dead, is it not to be wondered whether the presence of human life, as in these living cells, necessarily means the presence of the person? Obviously, there is human life in these tissue-culture cells, but the person is gone. Perhaps, then, the single-celled zygote at conception does not mean the presence of a new person at all.

This kind of thinking fails to recognize the difference between a cell that is part of a person and a cell that is a whole person. Even as sperm cells can be conserved for future insemination, cells from the surface of an adult's skin might well be conserved. Such cells are personal to the original individual; they can be said to be his or her cells provided, of course, that they have been continuously supported in their original, natural life. The donated organ is in no way, other than most figuratively, the organ of the donor; rather, it is specially structured matter that comes from the specific, living organ of the donor, and that now functions as an artificial organ. But while these individual cells are of a person, they are not a person.

The zygote, on the other hand, is the very origin of all other cells and parts of the living person. Each of the subsequent trillions of cells in the person's body came as a function of the zygote, and of no other single cell. Furthermore, the increase of cells that results from the zygote immediately tends toward the development of specializing parts in a highly organized unity, whereas the increase in a mere tissue culture exhibits no such tendency. If scientists eventually become able to stimulate artificially an ordinary cell of the body so that it undergoes the generative process, this new kind of human zygote would be another individual person with her own dynamic life-thrust and characteristics, radically other than the person from whom the pre-stimulated cell was taken, though much like that other person.

Not every cell or grouping of cells in the human body is a person. Only the whole of them can be considered to be the person, although every one of them is personal. But at conception, the zygote is the whole of the person's cells, the one in which all his other cells are potential, and through which they will differentiate. Trillions of a person's individual cells in all parts of his body die during his life, while he continues to live in and through new ones. With every one or many of these dying cells, we do not think that the person herself dies. None of these cells, in any way, approximates the dynamic and universal power of the zygote. If the zygote dies, the whole person, in quantity and in quality, dies.

The zygote is the only single cell that can be identified as a whole, living person. Not even the human brain can be so identified. The human person cannot be reduced to one or to all of his or her functions; not even to the function of their brain. Lack of brain development in prenatal life in no way argues for the absence of a person any more than does lack of arm development. Since the one-celled zygote is in no way part of a person, but is in every way a whole person, it is the only exception to the rule for all cells and organs of the human person, each one of which is part of a person, and not a whole person.

At the same time, it is false to say that the zygote (a whole person) is part of any other person. Some pro-abortionists try to say that the child in the womb is like a tonsils or an appendix, and that the removal of this prenatal life is similar to removal of tonsils or appendix. At the moment of conception, the new life has an entirely different genetic quality from any tissue of the mother's body. The same cannot be said about her tonsils or appendix. And neither tonsils nor an appendix has ever been known to become another person

.

## The Law of Continuity

Though the infant develops through many psychic stages from birth to adulthood, there is no basic change in his or her nature as a person. The same is true of his or her total development from conception to adulthood.

There are many years of difference between the adult and the child at birth. But there are only nine months of difference between birth and conception. If the long period of time and dramatic change between the infant and the old man does not entail a transition from non-person to person, there is much less reason why the very short period of development from conception to birth should entail such a transition. Birth is one stage in this long continuity.

Pro-abortionists who claim that birth is the beginning of human existence fail to recognize the fact that passage through the birth canal, followed by breathing and eating, is not anything like the depth of qualitative change that conception is. The beginning of breathing and eating simply changes the method of taking in what was already supplied in the womb, that is, oxygen and nutriment. But the being that does the taking in of oxygen and nutriment began at conception. Which is fundamental—the being that does the absorbing of oxygen and nutriment, or the different methods of doing this absorbing?

But some people would diminish the importance of the conception event by saying that there is also a basic continuity from sperm and ovum to fetus. They point out that the sperm and ovum, once they are released from the testes and ovaries, are just as autonomous with respect to the parents as is the zygote. They say that if cell-independence is the criterion for individual human life, the sperm and ovum are human beings as much as the zygote is claimed to be. But since it is preposterous to think that every one of the billions of sperm produced by a man, and the numerous ova produced by a woman, is a human being, they would insist that it is similarly unreasonable to regard the zygote as a human being.

This way of thinking overlooks the radical change in structure and dynamism that takes place at conception. Simply because the ovum and sperm are spatially and physically somewhat autonomous does not mean that they are qualitatively autonomous. An unfertilized ovum is still qualitatively a part of the woman, whereas the zygote is, in no sense, a part of that same woman. Thus, not until the ovum is fertilized by a sperm is there a qualitative change which brings into existence a new human being and the beginning of a whole new continuity which remains in every subsequent stage of development.

The unfertilized and the fertilized ovum cannot even be counted as one and the same entity. To suppose so would be to treat the conceptive process as if it were no different from that of rearranging furniture in a room; again a false reading of the artificial into the organic.

But some are saying that they will believe the fetus is human only when society has funerals in case of miscarriage. We could reflect more carefully on this point. We do not attend funerals of people we do not know, yet we recognize that the unknown dead were human persons in our midst. The embryo or fetal child is not even known by his mother. But though he is a stranger even to her, he is no less a person. The funeral is a social custom devised not so much for the people who leave us as for the people left behind.

## Person and Body

The human body, in all its parts and functions, is a revelation of the person's very being. Her so-called biological functions, such as breathing and the beating of her heart, as well as ovulation and the forming of sperm, are really personal processes that exist as internal revelations of her entire being. Furthermore, it is not the eyes that see, but the whole person who sees, in and through her eyes. Thus, an eye-specialist is a true physician only if he realizes that eyes are a revelation of a person's reality, and not just balls in sockets.

Though his body is an internal revelation of himself, the person is much more than his body. The energy of his being is not enclosed within the boundaries of his skin but opens into the world. As the earth is a concrete revelation of an energy-field that extends into the universe, the human body is the very being of the person revealing itself without enclosing the person within bodily limits. Thus, the person's body exists within his being. And the same is true concerning his body when he exists as a single cell having all his genetic characteristics. Again, the human zygote is not just a "genetic package" but is a one-celled person that has genetic components. The zygote is not just a potential human, but a human being with potential .

# CHAPTER 5:
# IS THERE ANY REASON
# FOR ABORTION?

Past defense of preborn life has been marked by serious weaknesses. Failure of the Churches to implement their convictions to the full, false conservatism in medical and hospital policies, and anti-feminist bias in male legislators, may well have occasioned pro-abortionist criticism. But these weaknesses do not set aside the point at issue: That the newly conceived being is an actual person and not just a potential person! Since there is no such thing as a potential person, only a potential personality, how can we best protect the newly conceived person from the onslaughts of ignorant or ill-willed fellow humans?

However, the failures of the Churches in this and in other areas of human life are not nearly as naive as those of many pro-abortionists. One of them, for instance, has asserted that "any woman knows the difference between the two-month-old-fetal tissue that is indistinguishable from menstrual blood, and the living, breathing baby she rears." Apparently no woman is supposed to care about, or want to see, the tremen-

42

dous difference revealed by recent science between the ovum which is simply a tiny part of herself and the zygote or embryo which is radically other than herself—a whole new human being. Apparently no woman is supposed to concern herself about the evidence supplied by high-powered microscopes. According to this evidence, conception brings into existence the kind of one-celled being that, by taking in nourishment, develops itself and gradually becomes more manifestly what it originally is.

## The Stand of the Church

In view of the grossly retarded concern for the preborn in the history of both Oriental and Occidental cultures, not to mention extended periods of acquiescence to infanticide, the Christian Churches have been a leading force in civilizing human awareness on the origin of the human person. It was only a hundred years ago that Pope Pius IX declared that the moment of conception must be held as the beginning of the human being. But this doctrinal improvement, however inadequately articulated and promulgated, was a truly progressive stride in the evolution of care and protection for our preborn fellow beings. And this teaching persists today in stark contrast to the regressive maneuvers of both civil and religious pro-abortion groups which deny the basic rights of prenatal humanity.

Moreover, even from earliest times, the moral teaching of the Christian Church opposed every form of abortion, at whatever stage of life, as a violation of the sacred process of human generation. Even during the period (12th to 19th centuries) when the theory of delayed ensoulment was in favor, the Church clearly opposed abortion from the time of conception.

This opposition to abortion did not depend, however, upon any clearly formulated statement of Scripture. Anyone who depends entirely upon the letter of Scripture is bound to miss much of its spirit. The Christian spirit of reverence for all human life, in whatever state of helplessness, has been the Scriptural basis for rejection of abortion. The absence of a prohibition in the letter of the New Law, does not always mean its absence in the substance of Christian Revelation.

Even when the mother's life is in danger, many Christian moralists hold that any direct attack upon the child to save the mother is prohibited. And the Christian ideal, "No greater love than this exists that one person give his life for another," strengthens this moral principle. However, the removal of a pregnant uterus in the case of cancer, or removal of a Fallopian tube that will rupture and hemorrhage due to a misplaced pregnancy in the tube, are not regarded by these moralists as direct attacks upon the child. In both instances, the surgery is performed to save the mother's life; it is undertaken in order to remedy a seriously defective condition in the mother, and not in order to produce an abortion.

## The Traditional Stand of the State

It seems, however, that a perfect sense of moral and Christian resolution cannot be demanded of the state in its civil laws. One exception to the moral law—abortion to save the physical life of the mother—seems legally justified. The child may appear to be an aggressor, though certainly not an unjust aggressor. Thus, the maternal exception stretches to its limits the principle of justice—a life for a life.

But now that this reason for abortion is outmoded by the advanced skills of modern medicine, many other reasons are being urged for legalized abortion. Our Constitution recognizes the necessity for taking human lives under certain circumstances that are determined by legislation. But these circumstances, based on the principle of justice as a life for a life, have always centered on the guilty—the criminal or the unjust aggressor. Are there any just reasons for taking the life of the innocent other than a matter of life and death? Are there any valid reasons for legalizing abortion?

## Rape and Incest?

In offering arguments for and against permissive attitudes on abortion, people can and do become quite emotional. Emotional arguments are not wrong in being emotional; but they may be entirely invalid because of their content or lack of content. In our thinking about the origin of human life and the abortion issue, we need all the refined and developed emotions possible.

The most emotional and persuasive plea for changing the law [1970] on abortion concerns rape and incest. But conception from rape is rare. Moreover, abortion for rape opens the door to any woman who would falsely allege rape. How could it be proven whether rape took place or not? The same is true of incest. When these tragic abuses actually happen, and when pregnancy results, there are two innocent victims: the assaulted and the newly conceived. If the young girl or woman were properly supported, she could rightfully be required to give nine months of her life to save the life of another innocent person. Then, if she is unable or unwilling to care for her child, she could give him or her to an adoption agency or an orphanage. In many localities, there are couples waiting to adopt a child.

The ultimate abuse is not sexual abuse, even though sexual abuse is horrible; it is extermination of the innocent. How can we respond to one form of abuse by inflicting a still greater violation on the other of the innocent victims? And what about the assailant? Should he be legally responsible for nothing?

## Physical Health?

Regarding abortion for the physical health of the mother, doctors say that any pregnant woman today, no matter what her illness, can be helped safely through her pregnancy, if she and her physician are motivated to make the effort. In our country, for instance, medical science already has advanced to such a point that this proposal for abortion is virtually obsolete. And everyone knows that the development of medical science is not about to come to a standstill.

## Mental Health?

Abortion based on the mother's mental indications is the next thing to abortion on request. Anyone who wants to terminate the life of an offspring is mentally disturbed. In cases of serious mental distress, women need emotional support much more deeply than they need abortion. Even a threat of suicide may be used as a kind of bluff, if not as a cry for help. The suicide rate among pregnant women is lower than among women in general. The mental health of the mother is a matter for social and legal concern, but surely it is not a valid reason for abortion.

Pro-abortionists are not beyond using for their own purposes the definition given by the World Health Organization that "Health is a state of complete physical, mental and social well-being, and not merely the absence of disease or infirmity." With a definition like this, is anyone healthy? Who, for instance, can know about the hunger, starvation, exploitation, indiscriminate killing of helpless people and the tenuous hold on life that all living beings now experience on earth, and still be in a state of complete mental and social well-being? Even to claim that one is, or can be, in such a state of well-being while fellow creatures and oneself are, individually if not collectively, on the brink of complete destruction, is to manifest the most un-healthy condition of all.

It would be much better to realize that we are all in a sick condition, in terms of the above definition at least, and to agree to help each other toward this ex-ceedingly distant goal of total health. Killing the whole of an innocent human life to save a part of the mental life of another is inevitably an act of regression in the total dynamics of healing the human condition. The mother's mental health is not a justifiable cue for an abortion.

**Prenatal Deformity?**

Finally, concerning the reason of prenatal defor-mity in the child it must be noted that there are many handicapped persons who live relatively happy and fruitful lives like the rest of us. The suicide rate among the handicapped is no higher than among others. Adults with mental health or medical disabilities do not consider themselves less worthy of continued life than so-called normal adults. Why should the presumption be any different for the fetal person who cannot yet think and speak for himself? Moreover, it cannot be known with certainty, in many cases, whether the child in the womb is deformed, or to what extent. Would it not be more "reasonable" to wait until he or she is born, have him or her thoroughly examined, and then destroy the child if he or she is too badly deformed? As medical science develops, many deformities can be reduced or corrected. Efforts should be invested in preventing and correcting deformities, rather than in promoting abortion.

Recent remarkable advances in the new science of fetology begin to constitute an ironic challenge to those who advocate abortion on the grounds of "fetal deformity." With fetal treatment and surgery taking place on a growing scale, the life and health of the prenatal person is having, at last, a social impact. People may begin to recognize that the fetus is a human being and a patient with as much right to life and health as his mother. A Look magazine article (11-4-69) states that until the advent of fetology the fetus was regarded by mothers, obstetricians and pediatricians as a quasi-living being; that until a few years ago the fetus was absolutely taboo; and that only in the last decade have doctors come to regard this attitude as nearly amounting to criminal negligence. However, the same article shows little awareness of the negligence of many contemporary physicians, psychiatrists and sociologists who advocate abortion where fetal deformity cannot be corrected.

# CHAPTER 6:
# ABORTION WITH LOVE

Does a loving concern for the victim of rape, or for the health of a mother, rightly lead to killing the unwanted? Is it a matter of loving concern to destroy a defective child to save him from a useless life? What are the implications of this so-called love?

In his book, *The Abortion Decision* (Doubleday, N.Y., 1969), David Granfield writes, "It would be naive for anyone to think that the compromise passage of a moderate abortion bill will do more than temporarily delay the fight for free abortion."

Granfield says that many former proponents of a moderate law are now its harshest critics because of their further support of demands for full permissiveness. Thus, restricted abortion laws, such as those allowing abortion to protect the physical and mental health of the mother, or for rape, incest and suspected deformity in the child, act as a foot in the door for abortion on request. A concern for the health of the mother readily becomes a demand for her absolute right to be free of any unwanted pregnancy. And a concern for the defective child readily becomes an insistent claim that no child should be allowed to suffer the

51

experience of being unwanted. Does this mean, then, that it might be 'necessary to destroy the child in order to save him?'

With the implication that abortion should be easily available, some have said that children have an inalienable right to be wanted by their parents. This is certainly true, but the child's right to be wanted places a duty upon his parents to want and care for him, rather than giving his parents the right to exterminate him. Thus, a Lutheran pastor in a New York slum puts it well when he says that by the criteria of smug middle-class abortion advocates, almost all the children of his parish should not have been born.

## The Urge to Kill

What seems to be an authentic concern for the welfare of mother and child is often a mask for a deeply rooted urge to kill. There is plenty of reason to believe that such an urge exists in the unconscious, if not conscious, life of human beings. How else account for wars, murders, and the brutal treatment of animals by some hunters, or even by children? It would seem that this urge, when it is suppressed in one way, begins to surface in another way. For example, many of those who protest the killing of innocent children in Vietnam promote, almost with a passion, the legalized attack upon the preborn. And many who oppose abortion defend the indiscriminate killings involved in warfare.

Like the ancient myth of Proteus, a god that could change into many different shapes, and who had to be held down firmly before he finally revealed himself for what he was, the urge to kill can change forms while remaining the same thing. This urge too must be firmly grasped so that it might reveal itself for what it is.

## Make Love, Then Kill

The most blatant irony of abortion-with-love appears in those who insist that they should have complete freedom to make love and terminate any unwanted intruder that results. But love with such an overkill as this is a lethal moral and public sickness. Women are being led to believe that full abortion rights will mean their ultimate sexual freedom. However, there can be no authentic freedom in human life without responsibility toward the lives of others involved in our actions.

# CHAPTER 7:
# HER NEW FREEDOM OR
# HER OLD SLAVERY

Though he revealed his insight in the form of a story, the author of Genesis, the first book of the Holy Bible, wanted to say that man and woman were meant to be friends, and that this was God's original intention, their Creator. But something went wrong between the man and woman–something very profound. As a result, all of human history has stumbled and groaned in suffering. Man develops the earth in a massive struggle; woman bears her children in painful labor. Finally, with a very penetrating insight into the human condition, the writer of Genesis reveals the most subtle of all results of the chasm between man and woman: "Your yearning shall be for your husband, yet he will lord it over you."

In this modern world "now come of age," the development of the earth is still a great struggle, childbearing is still a heavy responsibility, and women are still in subjection. Some time ago, Rep. Shirley Chisholm, a black woman in the United States House of Representatives, declared that it is more difficult to be a woman than to be black. The tension between blacks and whites is out in the open; it is not hidden in the guise of love. But the tension between man and woman, especially in marriage, is nestled in the guise of love. Few people can, or dare to, see it for what it really is.

It is true that women no longer are isolated from civilization as in ancient Greece. They are educated, have the right to vote, and can hold offices in the government. They are exploited and cheapened by commercials everywhere. In a vast "Playboy" subculture, women are treated as sex-objects and not as persons at all.

But women passively go along with the game. If they can have contraceptives, they believe they are free. Yet contraceptives are not enough anymore. Women everywhere are clamoring for their "ultimate freedom"—safe and legal abortion whenever they happen to want it done. And this they are calling "surgical contraception" and "fool-proof birth control." They are insisting that freedom from compulsory pregnancy is their inalienable right. Is everything that is compulsory unjust? Compulsory education? Compulsory taxation?

As human conscience becomes more sensitive, history may show eventually that the greatest killers have not been men with their wars, deathcamps and social purges, but women against their own indwelling children. Each year, millions of the most helpless and defenseless have been their victims. Yet, it is very noticeable that so many men never before have been so active in the cause of women's rights as they are for her "right" to become such a killer. One can easily see that this so-called ultimate freedom of woman is just another face of her age-old slavery.

## The Freedom to Choose How to be Used

When women insist that they should have the right to say how their bodies should be used, they are saying clearly enough that their bodies are being used, not only by new life, but more basically by those who begin this life. They fail to realize that persons are not meant to be used. But they allow themselves to be used, either tolerating it or liking it that way. And they naively think that abortion gives them the freedom to choose how this using shall be done.

Women themselves so often seem unconscious of the real root of the problem. In fact, the founding leader of the Planned Parenthood Organization, Margaret Sanger, has been quoted as saying that no woman can call herself free until she can choose consciously whether she will or will not be a mother. But what should be said about her freedom to choose in the face of undisciplined sexual passions which initiate the problem in the first place? The hyper-romantic notion of love in the Western world, and the idea that man is nothing but a high-class animal, are causes of the basic slavery involved. Is nothing to be done about these profoundly malformed ideas and their attendant emotions?

It is true that no woman can call herself free if she does not own and control her own body. But that control surely should include her conscious choice whether she will or will not engage in genital activity. The only problem is that few husbands (and, unfortunately therefore, few wives) would stand for that kind of freedom. Adult men and women in our society have not yet been weaned away from genital love-making as a necessarily regular occupation. Coital interaction is either disdained or idolized in the extremes of our Puritan-hedonist culture. People seem to be incapable of enjoying coital intercourse when it is proportionate to the circumstances, and of refraining from it when it is not proportionate to the circumstances. But the challenge of freedom, and most assuredly of genuine sexual freedom, inevitably confronts us all. Only a great people will accept this freedom and inherit its joyful fruits.

## The Underlying Sex-Problem

Abortion propagandists are fond of citing the exploitation of women by male legislators, as well as by the general cultural taboos on female independence. They seem to be completely unaware of their own encasement in this condition. By advocating the right of a woman to decide whether her pregnancy should or should not be terminated they tell her, in effect, that she cannot be expected to be responsible for her own love-making activity. She is thought to be too dependent upon man for that. The irony is that it is man, much more than woman, who is dependent on his own phallic drives and fancied "potency." Actually, the compulsive character of much of the male sex drive is not a sign of potency, but a symptom of a deep impotence in the individual person for creative control and for a broader, deeper sense of sexual love.

## The Age of the "Wanted Child"

One of the more articulate of the pro-abortionists calls the age of full permissiveness on this matter "the age of the wanted child." We need to call the bluff on this euphemism. What is meant by the wanted child of a killer-mother?

But one hears that words such as "kill," or "killer" should not be used in relation to abortion. These words are too emotional, it is said. Terms such as "legal termination of pregnancy" are more cool and objective. They are more medical and scientific. This is a strange sort of selectivity at a time when the slogan "Tell it like it is" is so popular.

At the moment of conception, a woman becomes a mother. And whether she knows it or not, a woman becomes a mother of a child. There are many facts that we do not know, even about ourselves, but they are facts, nevertheless. The human zygote is especially close to a woman's being; her womb is the first home of the new human person. Conception is the very beginning and foundation of motherhood. And the single-celled person has a right to his or her mother; he or she has a right to mother's womb, or else no one of us has a right to the womb of mother nature and of human society here on this planet!

What kind of woman kills her own child or asks to have him or her safely killed by someone else? Is she a person who accepts herself as a woman? Abortion is a woman's greatest act of self-hatred short of suicide; she attacks not only her child but also her own being as a woman and mother. Should she be given the legal right to violate her child and herself in this way? With her longing for freedom in her relations with man, should woman be allowed to vent her frustration on her prenatal child by exterminating her? Or should our society courageously begin to expose the root of this great evil?

*[Editor's note: God provides forgiveness and healing for women who have had an abortion. There are several ministries providing counseling to women scarred by abortion.]*

## Regression to Barbarism

Abortion, like human slavery, is one of the

world's oldest crimes. The Greeks and Romans had histories of abortion and infanticide. It is amazing that Christianity and other civilizing influences effected as much change as they did. Today's abortion proponents would have us return to the barbarous practice of total dominion over the prenatal person. They would have us shrink away from the evolution of human moral consciousness, through regressive notions of therapeutic efficiency and social utility. Where abortion is easily available, the minimal effort to use contraceptives, to say nothing of more human means of regulating conception, becomes less desirable. And the tragic slaughter increases year after year.

# CHAPTER 8:
# A RIGHT OF CONSCIENCE

Abortion promoters claim that the termination of pregnancy is a right of any woman's conscience, and that this should be a private matter to be resolved "in the sacred relationship between the woman and her doctor." But civil society does not allow parents to abuse their children in the privacy of their homes. If such cases are found out or reported, the parents are subject to prosecution, and rightly so. In a certain dimension of human life, each one's child is everyone's child. What should the law do, then, in the face of extermination, the ultimate act of child abuse?

**The Limits of Marital Privacy**

The right to marital privacy is not absolute. Even in the Griswold versus Connecticut case, the Supreme Court declared unconstitutional a law against the use of contraceptives, but it did not preclude breaking the zone of family privacy for "legitimate state interests." Surely the life and welfare of an unprotected fetal citizen is a legitimate state interest. The radical difference between preventing a human life by contracepting, and destroying a human life by abortion, however efficiently and painlessly done, makes the ruling in the Griswold case inapplicable to the abortion issue.

Moreover, the state is far behind in its responsibilities if it does not reach out and examine the various types of "contraception." Methods that are not clearly understood and that well may be abortifacient, such as the IUD (the intrauterine device) and certain low dosage drugs, must be ruled out of legitimate use. The "morning after" pill and certain injections, which are obviously abortifacient, are no longer to be labeled as contraceptives. They are as lethal to human life as are knives, guns, poisons and other not so tidy means of extermination.

## The Freedom to Do My Own Thing

One of the most insidious forms of rationalization offered as background justification is the characteristic plea, "I don't want to convince the majority that my way is right; all I want is freedom to do my own thing." Failure to distinguish carefully between those things that we can do on our own, and those things that cross the very limits of authentic freedom in a society of persons, will be the ruin of this civilization unless such a hyper-individualist attitude is modified. We must agree, for instance, that taking any other human life, no matter what age, race, religion, social status, state of health, etc., except that it be an occasion of absolute defense of one's own life, cannot be an act of true freedom. We must agree that anyone who makes murder his "own thing" will forfeit most of his own freedoms short of the right to life itself.

Presently, there is a strong awareness of the rights of conscience, along with little knowledge of the true nature of conscience. It seems quite clear that the birth control controversy, and its cry for the rights of conscience, have prepared people for leniency toward abortion. The idea that contraception should be a private matter of conscience, based on judgments of love, is being used in the plea for abortion on request. Perhaps this is one reason why many Christians, including many Catholics, are silent in the face of the abortion tragedy.

## Contraception and Abortion

Strictly contraceptive measures and abortion are radically different in what they do. But there seems to be an existential and psychological continuity in what they mean. Apart from the fact that most so-called contraceptives may well be abortifacient, (i.e., the IUD and low dosage pills) and that abortion is being called "fool-proof birth control," there is something about the meaning of contraception that disposes people for accepting or tolerating abortion. Implications tend to take their course whether people want to realize it or not.

When the human generative power is treated as a matter of sub-personal biology, it is easy to begin thinking that the result of this power, the child, is also a matter of sub-personal biology. After all, an effect can be no greater than its cause! It is logical to move from the idea that contraceptives control biology, to the idea that the human zygote, embryo or fetus is just biological tissue, and not a human being at all. The human power to give life is a capacity of the whole person through one of his interpersonal acts of communication, and this power is depersonalized when treated simply as a biological matter.

Not all people who advocate contraception would argue this way, but it may be instructive to listen to the thinking of one biologist who takes this position: any woman has an absolute right to procure an abortion "without giving any reason at all." He says that methods of contraception are improving so rapidly that we may have the "perfect" contraceptive before long, but even this will be imperfect if it requires any kind of foresight. From one hour of the evening to the next, he says, a woman does not know how she will behave. An 18-year old virgin does not know at the beginning of springtime how she is going to behave with her lover some time later. And a woman who is happily pregnant one month does not foresee the attack of an embryo-deforming virus the next month. Therefore, concludes this biologist, we will always need an afterthought method of birth control to take care of unforeseen contingencies. "Abortion is the much-needed backstop in the system of birth control." This classic piece of rationalization comes from the amoralism of one who himself rightly indicts ancient ethical and legal systems for having put women in a class "with children, idiots and slaves." But his whole thesis on abortion coordinates perfectly with the social thrust of the pro-abortion movement in the United States that treats women as though they were children with little or no foresight, as idiots without respect for the person of their own offspring, and as slaves of the passions of men, if not of their own passions as well.

## When the Dominoes Fall

If we have a low opinion of human beings as men and women, we will not maintain high standards for their conduct. In mating behavior, if we accept contraception without reservation, we dispose ourselves for accepting abortion as part of the birth preventive pattern. Where contraception is not recognized for what it is, it is extremely difficult to hold the dike of abuse at that point. But if contraceptive love is too private for our laws, surely the murder of abortion is a public outrage no matter how efficiently it is performed. An absence of any laws against abortion tells both men and women that they are constitutionally incapable of responsible romantic and familial behavior. And then if abortion, too, becomes accepted without reservations, it will be exceedingly difficult to prevent the dominoes from falling still further.

# CHAPTER 9:
# WERE THE DEATHCAMPS PROPHETIC?

Something from the depths of humanity came to the surface of Western man's history in the Nazi prison camps. Almost before anyone knew what was happening, there it was! Unwanted human beings were scientifically defined as creatures outside the class of humanity precisely because they were regarded as useless and unwanted. For the sake of a quality race, great quantities of persons were used up in tortuous work and then exterminated. But these horrors were promptly dispelled when the Allies moved in and destroyed the Nazi regime.

However, when a force in the human psyche surfaces and is forced down again, it continues to exist. If it is put out of memory or repressed, it continues to operate in the unconscious mind, and it may surface again in another form. Extremely unacceptable or painful events are the objects of repression. And the painful reality of the deathcamps is largely repressed or forgotten by Western man. We have not made the attempt to come to terms with the Nazi revelation. Better to forget it! It couldn't happen again, anyway! But, as Santayana once said, "Those who do not remember the past are condemned to relive it."

## Wanted and Unwanted

As things are taking shape in today's world, the preborn child is being defined outside the class of humanity, the better to dispose of him or her when he or she is unwanted. Promoters of abortion are telling us that we should be looking for quality in people and cutting down the quantity of people. They are saying that unwanted children, because they develop anti-social behavior, interfere with the quality of the race, and should be eliminated before they are born. Indeed, we should be dedicated to quality in human life, and we do hope that all children will be received in love. But the rapidly emerging idea that no unwanted child should be allowed to be born, and that no mother should have to give birth to an unwanted child raises a serious question as to the way in which children are wanted in our society. The possessive attitude toward children is just as destructive as the dispossessive. When the existence of a child is based so completely on the rights of a mother, what is her subconscious, if not conscious, attitude toward her wanted children? Actually, a woman who thinks she has an inalienable right to terminate any unwanted pregnancy is seriously damaged as a potential mother, though she may consciously think she wants the children she allows to be born, she is subconsciously destructive in her relation with these live children.

It is not only true that a child might threaten the mental health of his mother, but also that a mother can threaten the mental health of her children, even when they are wanted. Often, parents are amazed at what their children know about them. Children absorb much more from the attitudes in their environment than we realize. And they are sure to know that something is wrong with being a wanted child when an unwanted child can be done away with according to the mother's self-asserted rights. Then, if these so-called wanted children develop anti-social behavior, their parents are likely to say they cannot understand what went wrong.

Since an unwanted child may become later in life a dearly wanted child, and also since a wanted child may later become unwanted, abortion for unwanted pregnancy is something like cutting off an arm because of a headache or an eyestrain. It not only fails to reach the cause, but it monstrously complicates the symptoms resulting from sexual compulsion and pseudo-love.

Some moralists say that abortion is worse than ordinary homicide because it is done by mothers and doctors who are by nature sworn to protect human life. The truth of this view might be heightened by a comparison with a dishonest Judge. There is a special odium about a dishonest Judge because she is, as a Judge, sworn to be an agent of society in upholding the law.

## Creeping Legislation

*[A note to remind the reader: The book was written in 1970, and facts have changed since then. The abortion debate continues and evolves.]*

In states that have a modified abortion law, there are now well-organized groups agitating for full permissiveness. In California, where abortion was legalized in 1967, there is already a national committee for infanticide formed by a prominent San Francisco doctor. In England, a very permissive abortion law went into effect in spring 1968. Then in March of 1969, the Euthanasia Society presented to the House of Lords a bill for voluntary euthanasia that was defeated by a vote of 61-40. A too small majority! One of the members of Parliament has warned that legalization of voluntary euthanasia would precede pressures for involuntary termination of anyone thought to be a burden on society. He said that this point is far from speculative since there is now an increasing number of letters being published in newspapers from advocates of compulsory mercy-killing.

If a bill for voluntary euthanasia were passed, much could be done to put social pressure upon any unwanted person so that he might choose death "voluntarily." Stinging remarks can do much to instill feelings of being useless and undesirable. And attitudes can say more than words in effecting the same. Then, if people do not choose death voluntarily, pressures for compulsory euthanasia would be sure to follow. Where only the healthy and the productive person is safe, people would be afraid of becoming disabled in any way. The result would be an extremely neurotic society.

In his book, *The Abortion Decision*, David Granfield says, "It is impossible to vote for limited destruction of the unborn without justifying in principle the expendability of human life, all human life." Though this lethal principle might not be put into practice immediately, or fully, it does have an inner logic of its own. Some abortion promoters want abortion as the only form of life-termination. At the same time, they support unwittingly a principle of action toward human life that readily becomes applicable to other forms of life-termination. Where people are unthinking and apathetic, this falling-domino process, or the process of creeping legislation, can easily take hold. Long before the mass killings took place in the death-camps, says David Granfield, the ideological motivation, the legal structures and the institutional framework were ready and waiting. Things progressed by stages proposed in *Mein Kampf*. The deathcamps were "the logical, although not inevitable, development of earlier legislation."

In the explorative book, *The Terrible Choice: The Abortion Dilemma* (Bantam Books, The Joseph P. Kennedy Foundation, 1968), Dr. David Louisell, of the University of California School of Law, comments concerning the prospect of legalized abortion. He says that he will never forget the statement made by the Episcopal chaplain of the University Medical School when the abortion proposal came before the California Legislative Committee. The chaplain called attention to the conclusion of the film *Judgment at Nuremberg*, where the German Judge, in anguish, said to the American Judge, "Believe me, Judge, I never knew it would come to this." And the American Judge responded, "Sir, it came to this the first time you took an innocent life."

If this process of creeping legislation is set in motion again, it is likely to be more gradual, more sophisticated and more widespread than that of the Nazi regime. And it is likely to be based on a utilitarian philosophy which could be combined with political force. The Englishman John Stuart Mill said, "I regard utility as the ultimate appeal on all ethical questions." When utility becomes the ultimate appeal, rather than persons and their natural rights, persons become subjected to laws of utility. If they become "useless" or "parasitic" they might easily be defined outside the scope of moral concern. Would there be an army to move in and dispel this much more insidious oppression?

Ironically, the Anglo-American nations, and the United States in particular, are especially susceptible to utilitarian movements. We have no tradition of honoring the elders as valuable members of society. British and American philosophy is empirical, pragmatic and utilitarian with a vengeance; whatever works, and works immediately, is readily espoused as the solution to a problem. The universities are strongholds of language analysis, a philosophy that has nothing to say beyond logic and words, and that acts as a severe critique and repressive agent toward any other kind of philosophical thinking. In such an intellectual wasteland, there is nothing to prevent the utilitarian ethic from taking its dreadful course.

This is not the foreboding of prophets of doom; it is a studied awareness of the dynamics of repression. If repression can result in individual psychosis, it can also produce psychosis in a whole society.

## But It Won't Happen Here

[A second reminder. This paragraph precedes Roe v. Wade and in that sense, is prophetic.]

Already, at the time of this writing (1970), abortion is legalized in 15 or more of our states, with several allowing abortion on demand. In most of these states, mental indications in the mother greatly exceed all other reasons for life-termination. Many people are either actively promoting the abortion propaganda or passively failing to resist it. In a country that holds the right to life as the very foundation of its Constitution, and that gives the preborn a legal status, this is a most disturbing situation. Is there no reason for apprehension?

Elie Wiesel, in his autobiography, *Night*, tells of a man who escaped the slaughter of his companions by the Gestapo at a mass grave in Poland. This man returned to the Jewish community from which he had been deported to urge the people to save themselves. But no one would believe the horrors he told them; they labeled him a madman. Eventually, these people were deported to the deathcamps; they had not heeded the warning.

In his book, *Man's Search for Meaning*, Dr. Viktor Frankl, a psychiatrist who spent three years in Nazi prison camps, describes a similar unwillingness to believe the worst really can happen. This state of mind is called the "delusion of reprieve." He says that while the Jews were on the trains, and even while they were entering the gates of the camp, they "clung to shreds of hope and believed to the last moment that it would not be so bad."

In comfortable America, we, too, do not want to believe that the worst can happen. And even when sterilized slaughter is progressing in our midst, we want to believe that all will be well. Refusal to face and to counteract the imminent prospects of aseptic slaughter is not only repression, but the delusion of reprieve; we need to become aware of these defenses in ourselves. Most seriously of all, however, our refusal to face the abortion tragedy is due to a moral lethargy that cannot be excused by our repressions and delusions, or by any other psychic escape or defense.

# CHAPTER 10:
# NOW WE DECIDE

In reconsidering present legislation on the abortion issue, Americans today find themselves on a continental divide. Will we succeed in representing faithfully and proportionately all the citizens of our states, prenatal and postnatal? Will we recognize, celebrate and support the unconditional value of each human being at all costs, whether he is aged, maimed, undeveloped, or newly conceived? Shall we permit the capital punishment of the prenatal person whose only crime is that of self-development and survival, while we abandon such arrogant punishment for the cold-blooded murderer?

In 1960 the State of Wisconsin, on the basis of scientific evidence, amended its abortion statute by defining conception as the beginning of a human individual life. Mere opinion gave way to science. This was true progress! A Federal Court in that State declared part of the Wisconsin law unconstitutional so that abortions might be performed in the first three months of life. The Judge said, "We think it is sufficient to conclude that the mother's interests are superior to that of an un-quickened embryo whether the embryo is mere protoplasm, as the plaintiff contends, or a human being, as the Wisconsin statute declares." Thus, the progress made in 1960 was followed by a terrible regression. The Court statement implies that one person's special interests might have precedence over another's right to life.

<u>In the light of modern science, true progress on the abortion issue can be made only by taking abortion out of its archaic position in the category of felony and defining it, where it actually belongs, under our laws against homicide. In fact, if all present laws were repealed, abortion would immediately come under our laws against murder, and the guilty could be prosecuted for homicide. However, it would seem necessary to specify in our laws this particular kind of homicide and its related methods of detection and prosecution</u>.

At the time of this writing, the whole issue of abortion legislation is before the Supreme Court of the United States. Recently, this Court let stand without comment a decision by California's Supreme Court that the state's old law prohibiting abortion, except when "necessary to preserve" the mother's life, is unconstitutional on grounds of vagueness. It is true that the term "preserve" can be interpreted to include almost any reason for abortion. This action of the Supreme Court calls for the states to enact laws with more precise terminology; it does not prevent the states from making new, much more clearly defined and restrictive laws. In fact, Assistant Attorney General of New York, Joel Lewittes, says that in order to prevent the states from making laws to protect the lives of its prenatal members, the Supreme Court will have to be totally explicit in declaring that the human fetus is not a being that the state has a rightful interest in protecting. (Cf., Linda J. Greenhouse, "Constitutional Question: Is There a Right to Abortion?" *The New York Times Magazine*, January 25, 1970.)

However, if the Supreme Court explicitly decides that the state cannot protect the fetus as a human being and member of a minority group under our Constitution, it will be defying the numerous court decisions defending the right of the fetus to sue for injuries, to inherit property, and to receive medical care while in the womb on the grounds that this being is human. (Cf., John T. Noonan, "Amendment of the Abortion Law: Relevant Data and Judicial Opinion," *The Catholic Lawyer*, Spring, 1969, reprinted for distribution by the National Right to Life Committee, 1446 Duke St., Alexandria, VA, 22314.) It will also be defying the United Nations "Declaration of the Rights of the Child" which supplemented its "Universal Declaration of Human Rights." The Preamble states that "the child, by reason of his physical and mental immaturity, needs special safeguards and care, including appropriate legal protection before as well as after birth." (Declaration of the Rights of the Child, adopted unanimously by the U. N. General Assembly, plenary meeting, 11-20-59.)

Should the Supreme Court make such a disastrous move, it would be as guilty as any other agency of government or society in failing to defend innocent human life. With the consequent withdrawal of the educative power of law in the area of abortion, it would become still more urgently necessary to educate the people on the important difference between the legal and the moral. Not everything that is legalized is morally right. However, since civil laws should be based on moral laws, it is most desirable that legal structures defend a society's moral foundations.

If, on the other hand, the Supreme Court decides in favor of radical protection of the origins and continuity of human life from conception onward, then its action could be one of the most monumental and prophetic events in the course of human history.

## Let's Be Positive

When faced with the responsibility for protecting innocent human life, we must realize that truly positive legislation negates the negative as well as affirms the positive. In our law, we should be sure to represent the fact that abortion is always (even to save the mother's life) the classic negation of taking innocent human life. And we should be far more perceptive than our traditional laws have been in providing the positive grounds for our legal negation of abortion and in providing procedural safeguards for instances when this lethal act might be warranted.

The sentiment for abortion on request is so strong in our country that we are confronted with a new psycho-social Civil War over this issue. If, through repeal of present laws, or through compromise legislation which can be interpreted promiscuously, we break with the principle of a life for a life, then it will be extremely difficult to return to sanity. It will require a colossal effort to disengage our society from the attitudes and practice that will result. As will be shown presently, we are already over-committed to the destruction of the prenatal person, even under the traditional laws. We must not underestimate the power which, by unwise abortion laws, we would place in the hands of "liberal" abortion advocates once we minimally, but so really, yield. In this matter it is not enough to be liberal or conservative; we must be as radical as we are in protecting our own lives. Furthermore, it is questionable whether pro-abortionists are true liberals. They appear to be totalitarian in their insistence on the right to exterminate the innocent.

In preparing and enacting a new abortion law, we must not only consider the next five or ten years of legislative struggle. We need principles compatible with the best information and research in medicine, law, social science, and morality that will sustain us for centuries—principles which will deepen as our self-consciousness, individually and collectively, evolves.

As one contemporary sociologist wisely puts it, "The human condition has its heartaches that no legislation can alleviate entirely." But courageous adherence to the basic truths of humanity, despite the infection of utilitarian "ethics," is continually necessary in keeping human destruction and suffering at a minimum. The old statutes on abortion surely lack clarity and accurate provision of procedural safeguards. Yet these statutes have represented the basic conviction of our society that every person has a right to life and to equal dignity. At the time of their passage, legislative motivations may not have been entirely pure, nor medical knowledge and techniques as highly developed as they are today, but somehow the continental divide was vaguely perceived. Contemporary references of pro-abortionists to antiquated attitudes of 19th century lawmakers and judges toward the rights of women are true, but they beg the question whether the distortion of motivation invalidates the laws that resulted. Another red herring brought into the discussion is that our ancestors did not have a very refined notion of the separation of Church and State. This kind of argument insinuates that because certain religious bodies have vigorously opposed abortion that all serious opposition to abortion is religious; or that a person cannot oppose something both on religious and on civic or humanistic grounds. Besides this one, there are many other distracting arguments offered to hide the basic truth of civilization that is involved in the question of life and death for the prenatal human being.

## Falsely Positive Legislation

Purity or impurity of motivation aside, once we cross the threshold of legislation on grounds of health in the mother or deformity in the child, for instance, then we are as guilty of the death of the innocent, as those who would permit abortion on request. So-called "moderate" legislation has already proven to be a step on the way toward repeal of all legal protection for prenatal lives. Since there is no middle ground for compromise between life and death, middle-of-the-road or compromise bills have no ground on which to hold themselves in place. Permitting abortion at any stage from conception onward, in cases of deformity in the child or a serious threat to the health of the mother, to say nothing of rape and incest, cannot be interpreted as positive legislation. It is negative legislation. Such willingness to legalize the unjust killing of even a single human being, in principle as well as in practice, can only bring the judgment of future generations down upon us, something like that which we visited upon the defendants in the Nuremberg trials. Approving legally and in principle the destruction of even one innocent human life is a price too high to pay for the support of any esteemed medical, legal or social organization.

Negations in positive guise are to be found in traditional legislation that defines pregnancy not by conception but by implantation in the uterus. Thus, the D & C (dilatation and curettage) permitted after rape is thought to be one of preventing pregnancy, since it prevents implantation. But the mother is essentially pregnant with a child, or with children, as the case may be, before the growing human being finds it necessary to differentiate for itself a special organ of nutrimentation and waste elimination (the placenta) in order to proceed toward higher stages of development. The act of implantation in the womb surely is no more nor less necessary to the developing being than is the shedding of the placenta necessary to the emerging child at birth.

Were scientific technology to provide a chemical which would kill sperm but not the zygote, then application of this contraceptive would be legally warranted. Otherwise, when we merely rationalize that the chances of conception are rare anyway in the case of rape, and that we are simply removing the offending sperm, we reveal our willingness to take innocent human life. We seem to be admitting that we are willing to kill very definitely, if only indirectly, by removing the lining of the womb, the beginning human being should such result, even though the equally innocent life of the mother is not in imminent danger.

How much difference is there between directly shooting a person, and willfully depriving him of all food and liquid?

Apparently, human consciousness has not yet evolved to the point where medical decisions are based on the fact of possible pregnancy rather than only on actual pregnancy. For example, curettage is a common gynecological practice. And physicians do not avoid the second half of the menstrual cycle when a zygote might be about to root itself in the uterus. Nor are women scheduled for curettage instructed to avoid coitus (Hellegers, op. cit.). This is evidence of primitivism in human consciousness and conscience, which future professionals surely will look upon with disgust. If possible pregnancy has no meaning, then it is little wonder that actual pregnancy is so willfully destroyed.

**Truly Positive Legislation**

Truly positive legislation on the abortion issue would seek to alleviate the deplorable conditions surrounding the birth of unwanted children. Our government should encourage research into the prevention and correction of prenatal defects, give aid to parents who nurture and educate handicapped children at home, directly subsidize the education and necessary care of the handicapped, provide free counselling and psychiatric care for unfortunately pregnant women or girls and their families, educate in responsible family planning including the responsible care of the initially unwanted, encourage medical research into the prospects of fetal transplantation in cases of extreme maternal unwillingness and initiate anti-poverty and other social programs oriented toward personal care that would ease the compulsion toward abortion. The relaxation of the law against abortion is a false solution that can only weaken the public attitude toward the dignity and value of human life, and hasten the social and moral deterioration of the total civic community. At least equally important as government support through legal and fiscal means is the need for private initiative in remedying the social problems connected with the demand for abortion.

A magnificent example of personal initiative in lessening the demand for abortion is Birthright, an organization founded by Louise Summerhill in Toronto. By means of an ad in the daily paper supplying a phone number [and now at https://birthright.org], many desperate women and girls find the counseling and understanding needed to help them through their pregnancies. This organization is based on the conviction that the child has a right to be born, and that his mother has a right to let him or her be born (Cf., Roger Keene, *Maclean's*, May, 1970).

Furthermore, the rapist should be fully liable for the support of his child, at least financially according to his means, until that child reaches the age when she can care for herself. The expansion of resources in both civic and private adoption agencies should also be encouraged. Adopted children surely receive better care than they would in the home of their own rejecting parents who would neglect or otherwise abuse them. And adoptive care is infinitely better care than would be forthcoming from those who argue for prenatal execution, namely, no care at all.

Truly positive legislation on this issue would also take a stand against the human negativity of prenatal murder. The traditional laws have not been positive enough. They do not attend fully to the scope of this inhumanity to man. They are based on somewhat outmoded concepts of the human person, and certainly on outdated knowledge of the medical and biogenic dimensions of human life. They need a truly evolutionary development, through which the law can become fully attuned to an increasing sense of value in human life and to an increasing knowledge of its origin and development. As this society rockets into the fantastic future of genetic engineering and cybernetic control, our laws must become far more differentiated and sensitized both in substance and in methods of defense. Second-rate measures on abortion are basically negative, and only postpone the crucial work of radical revision that will be necessary to preserve a free society for the future.

# CHAPTER 11:
# PROHIBITION

Another Case of "Prohibition"?

It is all out of proportion to compare abortion laws to alcoholic Prohibition Laws, as some have done. A better comparison with Prohibition Laws would be laws against contraception. But legalized contraception, when it is truly contraception, and not a method involving the direct or indirect destruction of the human zygote or embryo, is radically different from abortion. Even though some might consider legalized contraception to be detrimental to society, something akin to the legalization of not entirely innocuous drugs, there is no honest comparison between preventing conception and the deliberate destruction of an already conceived person by abortion.

Depending upon the social climate of the time, certain laws may or may not help to regulate the use of potentially harmful agents. But no genuinely free society can long sustain itself as such once it willfully refuses to recognize the right to life of each and every human being within its care.

Unlike contraception, abortion is a capital violation of the person of another by one or both of parents and by the society that permits it. A truly positive and progressive abortion law will sharply discriminate between preventing conception and preventing implantation in the womb by means of devices and chemicals that are known to be or suspected to be abortifacients. These devices and chemicals will be not only outlawed, but their removal from the market will be rigorously enforced. Such a sophisticated protection of innocent human life, in view of advanced knowledge of its genesis and development, and in view of the much more complex problems rapidly developing in connection with genetic engineering, chromosomal manipulation, cloning, artificial gestation, etc., is only proportionate to the circumstances and could be properly called progressive.

# CHAPTER 12:
# THE EDUCATIVE
# POWER OF LAW

The true test of an abortion law is not the number of offenders it prosecutes, but the number of abortions it prevents. The traditional law has kept down the number of prenatal deaths. When more permissive statutes were enacted, legal abortions increased without a reduction in illegal abortions. Though the traditional law is still grossly undeveloped, it has committed our society to a high regard for human life, and it has exercised enormous educative power. (David Granfield, op. cit.)

The teaching power of a law that does more than relate to matters of social taste, but reaches into the foundations of the society itself, can be tremendous. Even a lack of perfection in its enforcement does not render it useless or argue for its repeal. For example, civil rights laws have been a tremendous educative force even though they are difficult to implement. Murder laws for the protection of the ordinary citizen are difficult to enforce; many killers go unprosecuted. Each year the crime rate soars. Should these laws therefore be repealed?

It is true, however, that grave weakness in enforcing the abortion law does minister to lack of respect for law in general. And it is also true, as pro-abortionists say, that the least affluent, and the least "well-connected" individuals are discriminated against when physicians quietly break the law in state or private hospitals for certain "therapeutic" indications. Such hypocrisy should be rectified, not by impartially acceding to the requests of all, but by equally denying the requests of all who seek one of the greatest acts of social hypocrisy: abortion-with-love.

Some abortion opponents have been infected by a fear that the social hypocrisy of illegal abortion will lead to the even greater legislative hypocrisy of allowing abortion for certain specified reasons. They think it would be better for the state to withdraw protection from all fetuses during the first 20 or so weeks of their existence, thus keeping the state out of the business of deciding who may live and who may die before birth. But this proposal would allow the state to forsake its obligation to preserve and protect innocent human life. Such would be abortion-without-noticing: another form of social hypocrisy.

The movement toward repeal of abortion laws has been described by some people as one aspect of the civil rights movement. And many physicians, legislators, scientists, moralists and ordinary citizens have fallen for this claim. On the contrary, civil war for the rights of enslaved black people presumably concluded over 100 years ago. But the implementation of this people's hard-won freedom is only now beginning to take hold. In the meantime we find the emergence of the new slaveholders, the new class of Americans both white and black who demand the "freedom" to say yea or nay to the very life of their own preborn children, whom they conveniently define outside the class of humanity.

Never before has this nation yielded legally on the principle of preserving manifestly innocent human life. Even more crucial than the violation of defenseless people's freedom of opportunity is the violation of the right to live. A fetal power movement can hardly be expected. In this area of oppression, even more than in others, concerned citizens will have to defend the right to life as essential to a truly pluralistic society. Is it not utterly preposterous that the richest nation in world history, in her most affluent period of existence, is rising up against the rights of her prenatal members?

Laws are more important for what they mean than for what they do. This is why we must have great respect for the power of law to educate the attitudes of the people. Anyone aware of the psychic life of human beings knows that the subconscious mind is educated as much as, if not more than, the conscious mind. Mental life beneath the surface of awareness is like the largest part of an island beneath the surface of the water. What does the law say to the people in that part of their minds which is always active whether they realize it or not? A law that defends the rights of the preborn to life says that all innocent human life is inviolable. And a law that allows for the extermination of certain unwanted lives in the womb really says that all innocent human life is less valuable.

If we have no inalienable right to life from the time of conception, is there any other right we can really have?

If we as a people, do not take a strong stand at the beginning of human life, with all its implications for the rest of human life; if we do not care about our prenatal brothers and sisters, the death-camps may well have been prophetic!

# APPENDIX

## TWO KINDS OF POTENCY

Pro-abortionists often claim that the human zygote, embryo or fetus is only a potential human being. But there is no such thing as a potential human being, only a human being with potential. In order to understand this, a careful analysis of the meaning of potency is necessary.

Of the two radically different kinds of potency, there is the potency to cause something to come into existence, and the potency for the new being to become fully what it is. This latter kind of potency applies only to living things, since only these can grow or become more manifestly themselves. Moreover, the ovum and sperm especially manifest the first kind of potency: the potency to cause something to come into existence. And the zygote especially manifests the second kind of potency: the potency of an existing being to become more expressly what it already is.

## A Source of Confusion

One of the important sources of confusion regarding these radically different kinds of potency is the fact that they interweave. The potency to cause something to come into existence, which is proper to the ovum, for instance, also entails the latent function of disposing the newly caused being (the zygote) to become fully what it *is* once it is. And once the zygote is, its potency to become fully itself, also entails the latent function of internally causing its own stages of organization and development. Nevertheless, these potencies should not be confused, and should be understood as being radically different between gametic and zygotic cells.

The ovum, for instance, besides having the potency to cause, together with the sperm, something else to come into existence, also has its own potency to become fully itself once it is. And this potency is attained at the very beginning of its existence. The potency of the ovum to become fully itself, as an ovum, includes its capacity for containing 23 chromosomes, as well as its capacity for causing, together with a sperm cell, a new human being. Moreover, this new human being, the zygote, has its own radically different potency for becoming what it is once it is. And within its potency for becoming what it is is its potency for causing embryonic, fetal, infant, child, adolescent and adult stages of development.

## A Clarification

In brief outline, the complex situation is something like this. A man and a women, through their sex cells, have the power or potency to cause another human being. The woman's ovum, for instance, can be said to be a special and indispensable instrument, or even itself a cause, in this causal process. But the ovum in no sense, except in the most figurative and misleading, can be said to become a zygote. Nor do the ovum and sperm together become a zygote. The ovum and sperm become not only potential but actual co-causes of the zygote. In doing so, each of these cells, ovum and sperm, fulfills one of its own original potencies for becoming fully what it is: a causer of a new human person. But neither one of them, nor both together, become a zygote. The unique genetic identity of the zygote is not reducible to that of the ovum or the sperm, taken either separately or together. The 23 chromosomes of the ovum, for instance, are not simply added to the 23 chromosomes of the sperm. That would be too much like adding legs to a seat in order to make a chair: a projection of the artifact again! There is a dynamic transformation involved. The new being that results naturally contains many similarities to its parental elements, but is not, even in part, identical with either of these cells, or with both of them together. As said before, it is false to think that the zygote is a series of chromosomes. The zygote is a unique human being who has the unique chromosomes caused by his parents.

Though a child may be similar to his parents, he is, in no sense, identical with either one, or with both of them together. What is so obviously true between child and parents, as developed persons, is much more radically true between the zygote cell that is a new person and the causal cells (ovum and sperm) that never were and never can be persons, not even potentially. Many people have experienced in marriage that their union is something greater than the individuals themselves, even while they remain fully themselves. When the individual cells (ovum and sperm) do not even remain themselves in their union, but go out of existence in causing an entirely new being, how much more radical is the result of their causal union than the very union of marriage itself?

Thus, there is no such thing as a potential person, except when speaking figuratively. This manner of speech too easily becomes a tragic smokescreen serving variously the vested interests of ignorance, prejudice, indifference, malice and utilitarian attitudes toward the prenatal human being.

# AFTERWORD
by Mary Joyce

How we think is how we live. If we think, as Psalm 8:5 says, that we are "a little less than the angels," we would not be living in so much darkness of mind and heart. A little less than the angels is not a rational animal as the ancient, still used, definition of our human nature says.

We can be rational if we know how to think. But we are persons, not animals. Every cell in our body is the cell of a person. And that is as true about the single cell at conception as it is true at every stage of human life. Otherwise our thinking becomes superficial instead of natural. And even though we are creative, such as inventing helpful and useful things, we need to respect our human nature. That is what it means to be a human person.

Even though our Declaration of Independence specifically defines life as an unalienable right, the Supreme Court turned our United States Constitution against human life before birth because it was not explicitly mentioned as protected. Heavy pressure was surfacing from the growing Playboy culture with its lower-than-primitive view of human sexuality.

*Afterword by Mary Joyce*

As young people learn more about human life before birth, and as they realize that their own life could have been freely taken from them, and as more people see pictures of life before birth and change their mind about abortion, these hopeful trends could lead both our culture and our nation's Constitution into the transforming light of life.

# ABOUT THE AUTHOR
By Maureen Clements Dahl & Doug Dahl

## Mary Rosera Joyce: The True, the Good, and the Beautiful

As classic liberal young turks in the Pro-Life Movement in the early 1970s, we amazingly became philosophical protégés of Bob and Mary Joyce. Their books, including *Love Responds to Life* and *Let us be Born*, formed much of our apologetic in defense of the preborn. They took our visceral response to the horror of abortion and, along with like publications from other great authors of the time, formed it into a coherent and rational, yet no less passionate, case for the sanctity of human life.

Mary Rosera Joyce was born in Coleman, Wisconsin, in 1930, and grew up as a Wisconsin farm girl. As the eldest of ten siblings, Mary learned early to treasure small children, to shelter and care for them, as she did in her unofficial teenage role as the town babysitter in Lena. Mary was gifted as a writer, poet, and painter, as well as a musician who could sing and play the piano and organ. As a young teen she wrote a four-thousand-line poem entitled "A Tale of the North Wind."

She married her best friend, Robert Joyce, a Notre Dame student and subsequent Philosophy Professor at St. John's University, Collegeville, MN, while Mary taught at the College of St. Benedict nearby.

Mary deeply revered Bob, a man of extraordinary breadth of thought and feeling. She makes it clear that her achievement in the prolife movement was in a large part due to her husband's extraordinary energy and commitment. And together they amplified their effectiveness as advocates for life.

In 1968 they became one of the earliest founders of Minnesota Citizens Concerned for Life, the largest and one of the most successful state prolife organizations in the nation, boasting more than 200 local chapters. Mary and Bob laid the foundation for MCCL by traversing the state forming local pro-life groups, writing newspaper editors, and recording radio commentaries in support of babies in the womb. Together they authored the first book of the prolife movement in 1970, *Let us be Born*, which was distributed free to every attendee at the first National Right to Life Committee convention.

Mary's courageous actions were spurred on by her teenage aspirations. Even at the young age of 16, Mary thought philosophically and dedicated her life to the ultimate desires of mankind, called the transcendentals of being–the true, the good, and the beautiful, a commitment that reflected itself in all her subsequent work. She went on to write numerous books including *Love Responds to Life, Women and Choice, The Future of Adam and Eve, Friends for Teens,* and *How Can a Man and Women Be Friends.*

There is no better descriptor for her many books than the words of that commitment to the true, the good, and the beautiful. At 90 years of age, Mary continues to write, and bring joy to the 50-year friendship we've built with this remarkable lady. Hers is truly a life well lived, and a treasure to cherish, as she has spent her life cherishing the preborn. Bob's words and thoughts live on in *Let us be Born*, and we treasure the hope of his renewed friendship in the resurrection.

—

*Maureen Clements Dahl was co-founder of SOUL—Save Our Unwanted Life, a student youth and campus prolife organization at the University of Minnesota in the 1970s, and co-organizer of the National Youth Prolife Coalition.*

*Doug Dahl served as Assistant Director of the Human Life Center, St. John's University in 1976, and also as an MCCL staff member, and Assistant Director of American Citizens Concerned for Life.*

# ADDITIONAL BOOKS AND WRITINGS

by Mary and/or Robert Joyce.

Some of Robert and Mary Joyce's books are available online at https://www.meaningforbeing.com.

Let us be Born

# THE IMPORTANCE OF HOW WE THINK

An interpersonal relationship is between subjects, including the one between self and God. Between two persons for whom the other is an object, their relationship is impersonal. When this happens between us and God, atheism becomes possible.

Why, then, is this problem growing in our culture today? We have only to notice how secular media makes an object of anyone, everyone, and everything. The preborn child is even an object for the mother. How can she believe in God if she cannot believe that her own child within her is her child, but is instead an unwanted object to be removed? Being objective in a world of objects is not a wholesome condition for the human mind.

Many of us do experience in prayer a subject-subject, interpersonal, relationship with God. But some of us are thinkers and writers who relate to God as an object. Philosophers and theologians are among them. They are the ones in danger of objectifying God too far for having any love in their heart and soul, and so becoming potential, if not yet, atheists.

Theologians and philosophers, therefore, and especially scientists, need to develop their intersubjective relationship with God if they hope to avoid a trip into darkness. Remember Socrates! He turned his back on the gods when he started his journey into philosophy by making justice an object of his attention. This does not mean that he needed those particular gods, but he did need the one true God, who was unknown to him at the time.

In the desert of Sinai, however, Moses heard the greatest words ever spoken: "I Am Who Am" (Exodus 3:14). Wonderfully, we are called to an intersubjective relationship as was Moses with the Divine Being later revealed as One God in Three Divine Persons and no one of them an object for the others. They were then, and are now, and will be forever, intersubjectively one God. And we are called to a creature-Creator relationship with them for eternity. Nothing could be more wonderful.

Why, then, is the subject-object relationship still in charge and feeding separation from God? There must be something we are supposed to know, and do not know, because of our subject-object mentality.

We need a new way of thinking about relationships. Since it cannot be between objects nor between a subject and an object, it needs to be between subjects. This is where a different kind of thinking is required. It is a subject-subject or intersubjective way of seeing and thinking. This is where we are truly an image and likeness of God. The Divine Persons are infinitely intersubjective: our relation with them needs to be finitely intersubjective, especially in prayer and contemplation. A relationship with God that is objective only is impersonal, and lacking in faith, hope and love.

– Mary Rosera Joyce
Spring, 2021

# Your being has meaning!